MAGICAL MANDALAS
ADULT COLOURING BOOK

Paul Andrew Smith

©Paul Andrew Smith 2020

All rights reserved.

Relax and unwind with this amazing collection of intricate mandala designs for you to colour. Beautiful patterns to use your creativity and artistic talent on.

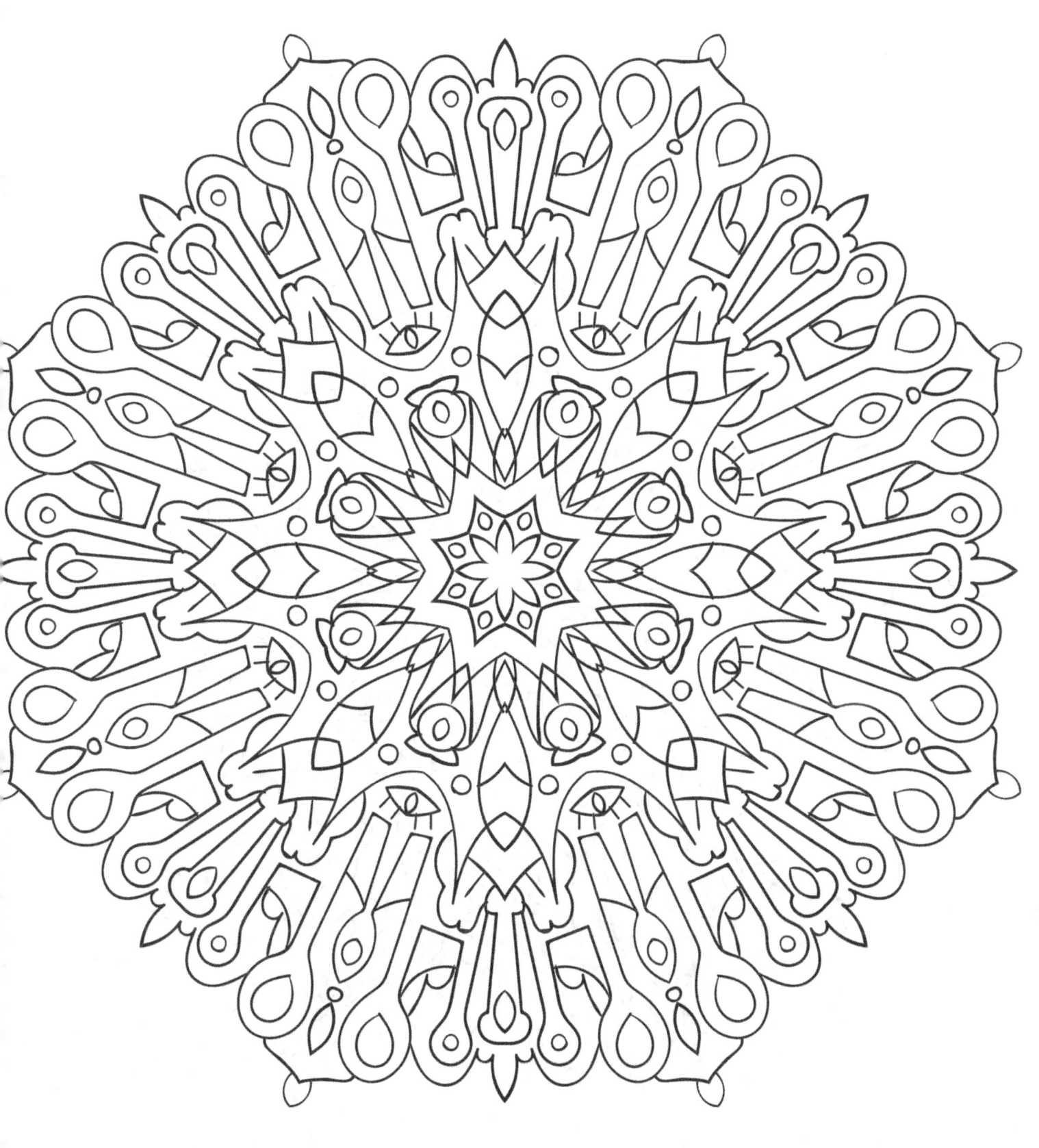

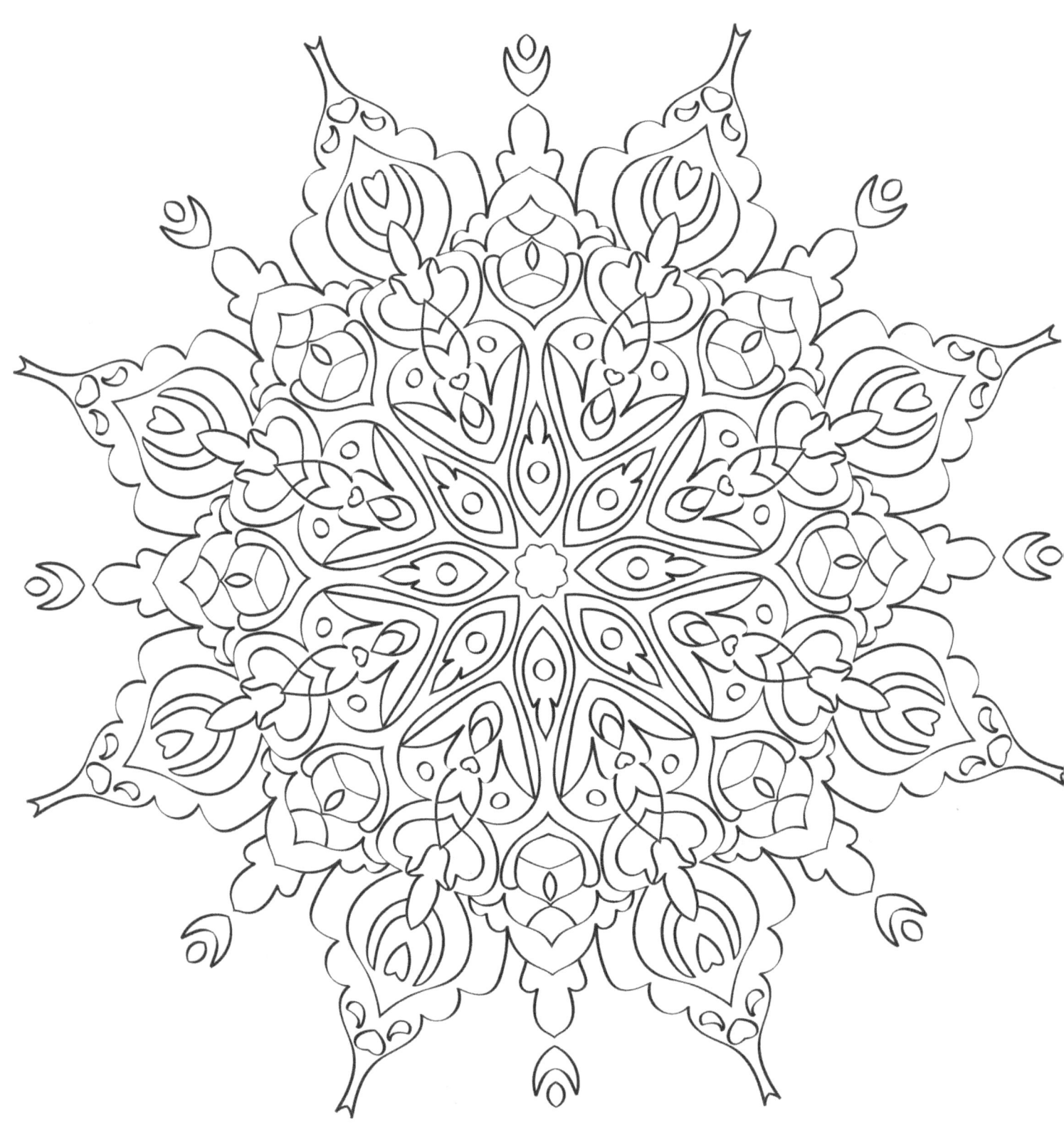

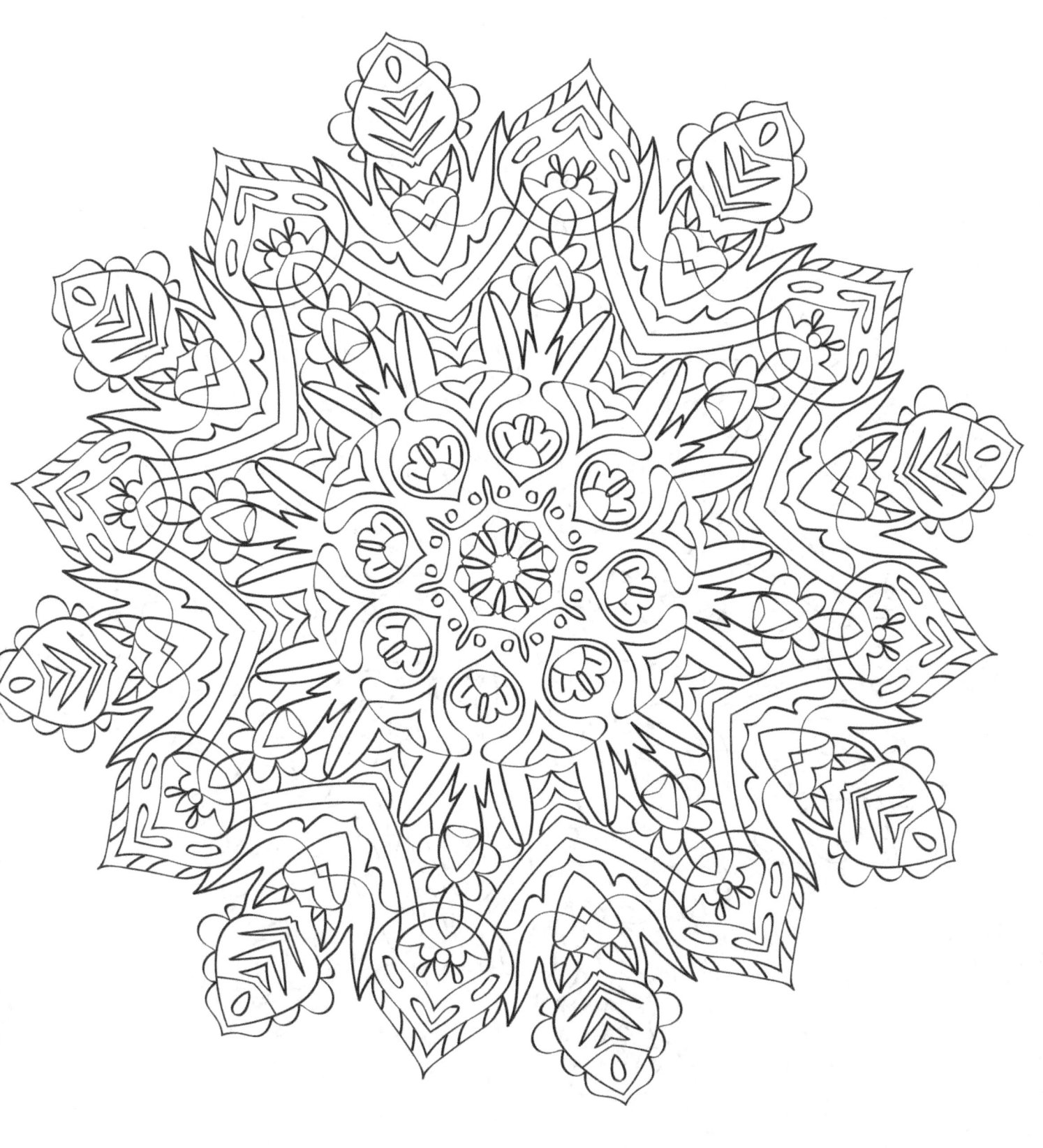

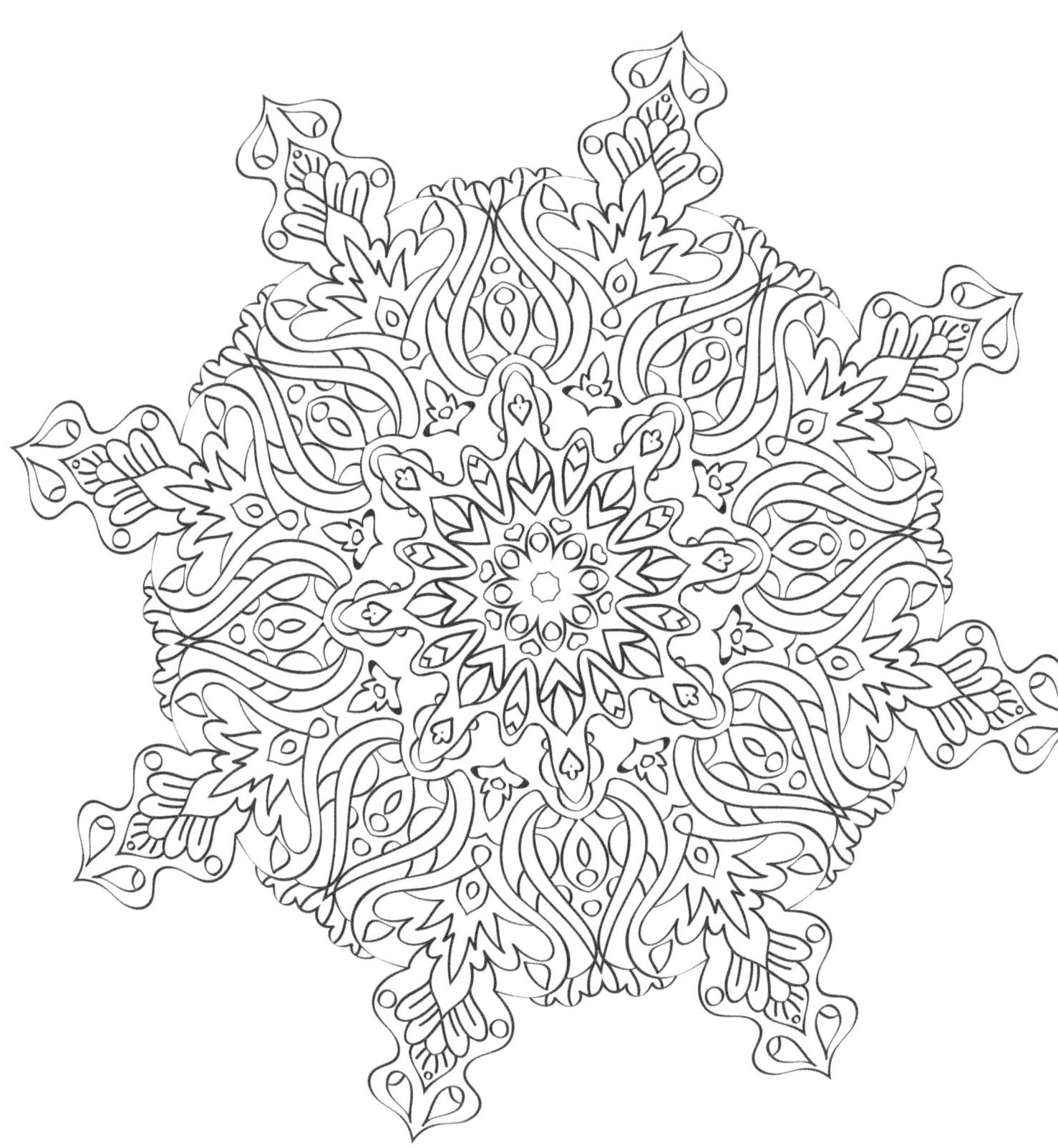

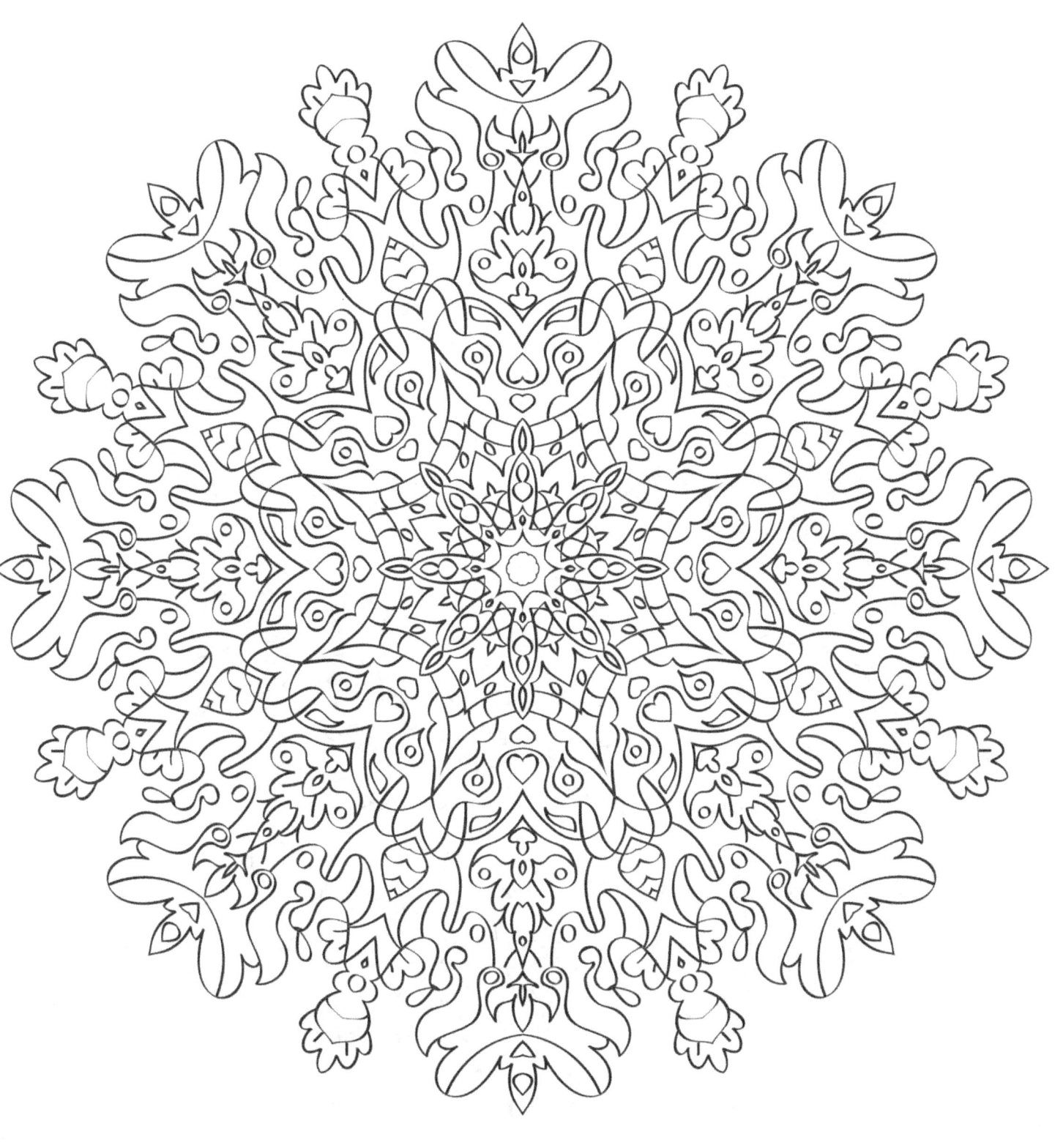

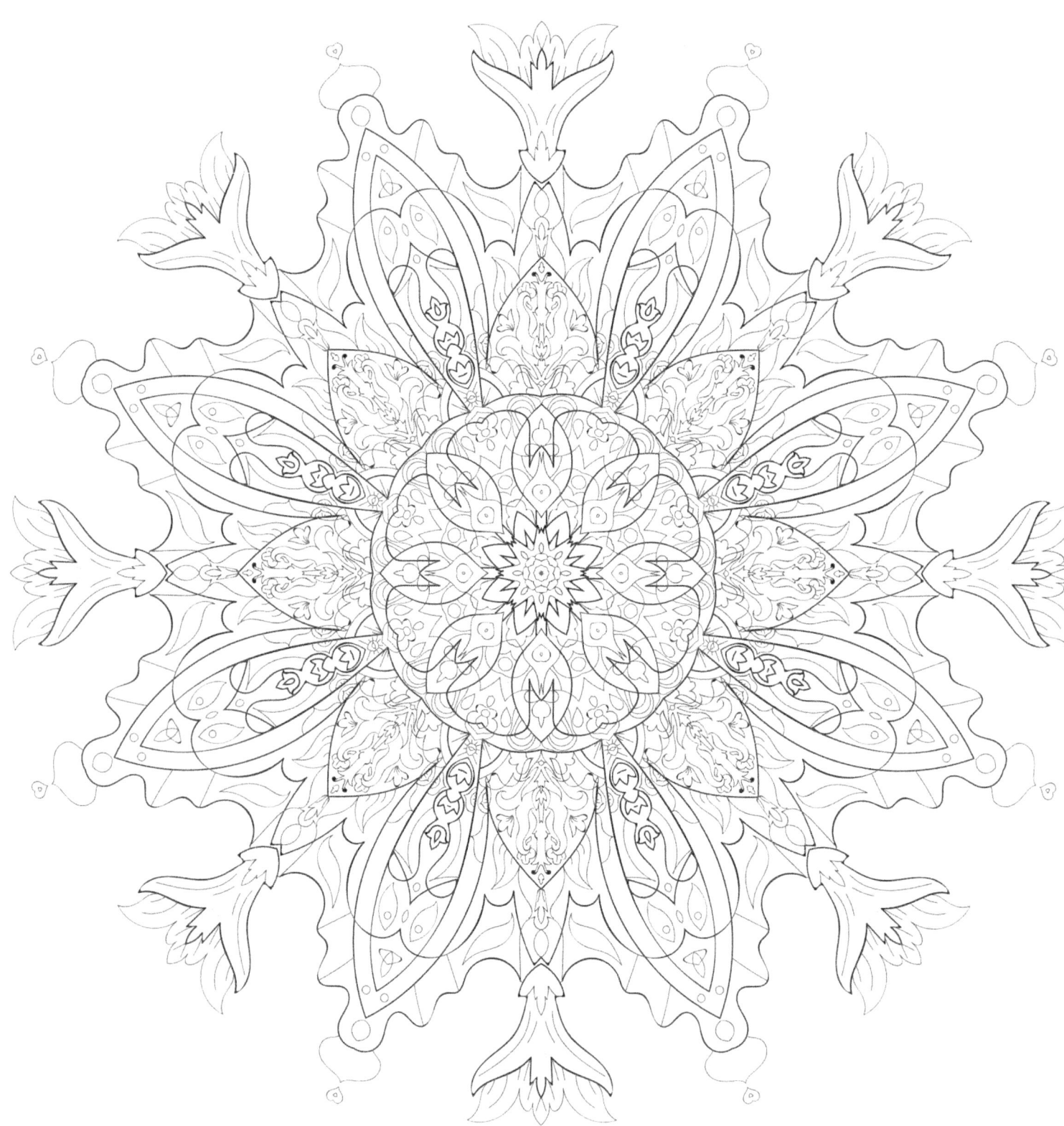

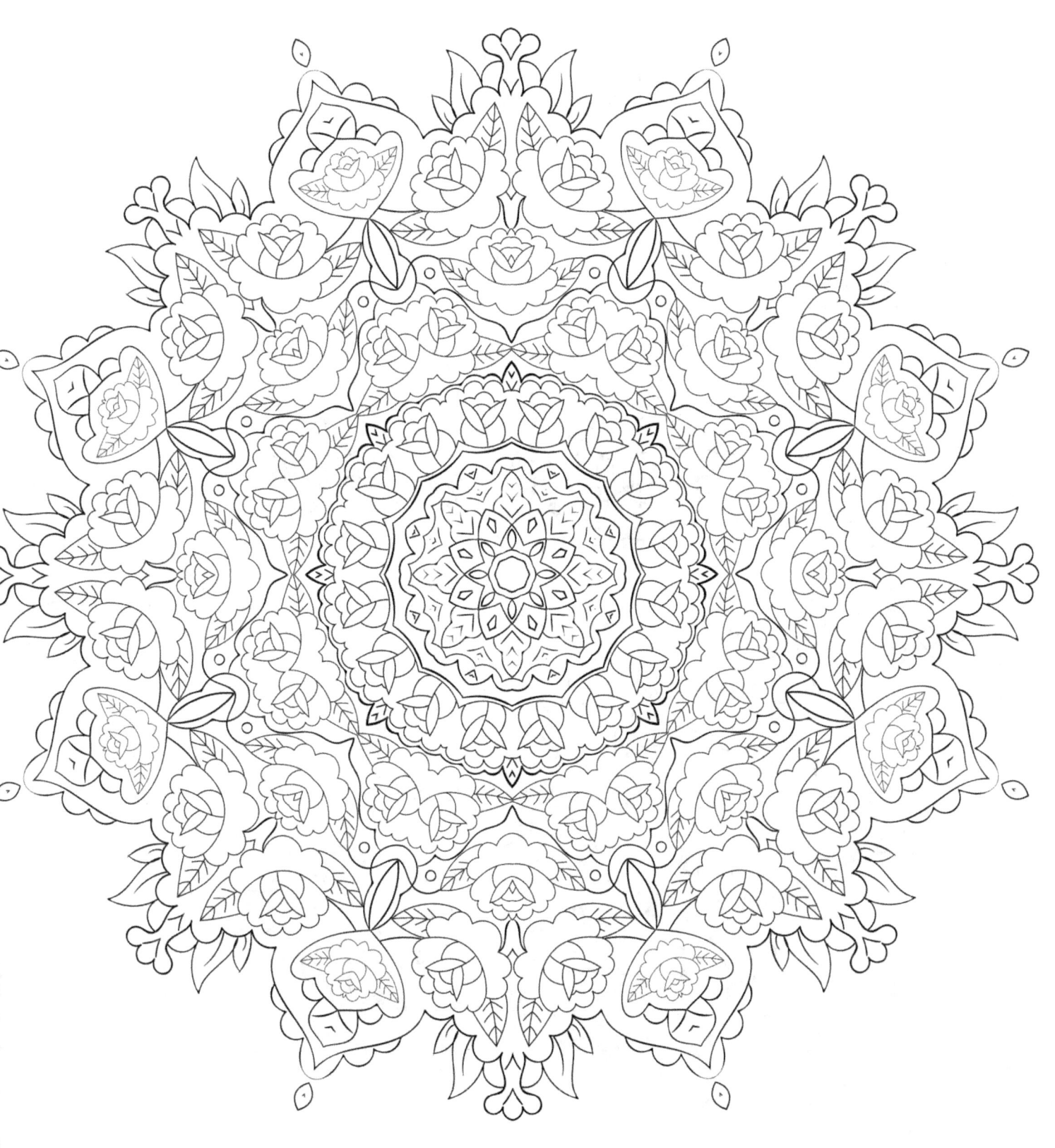

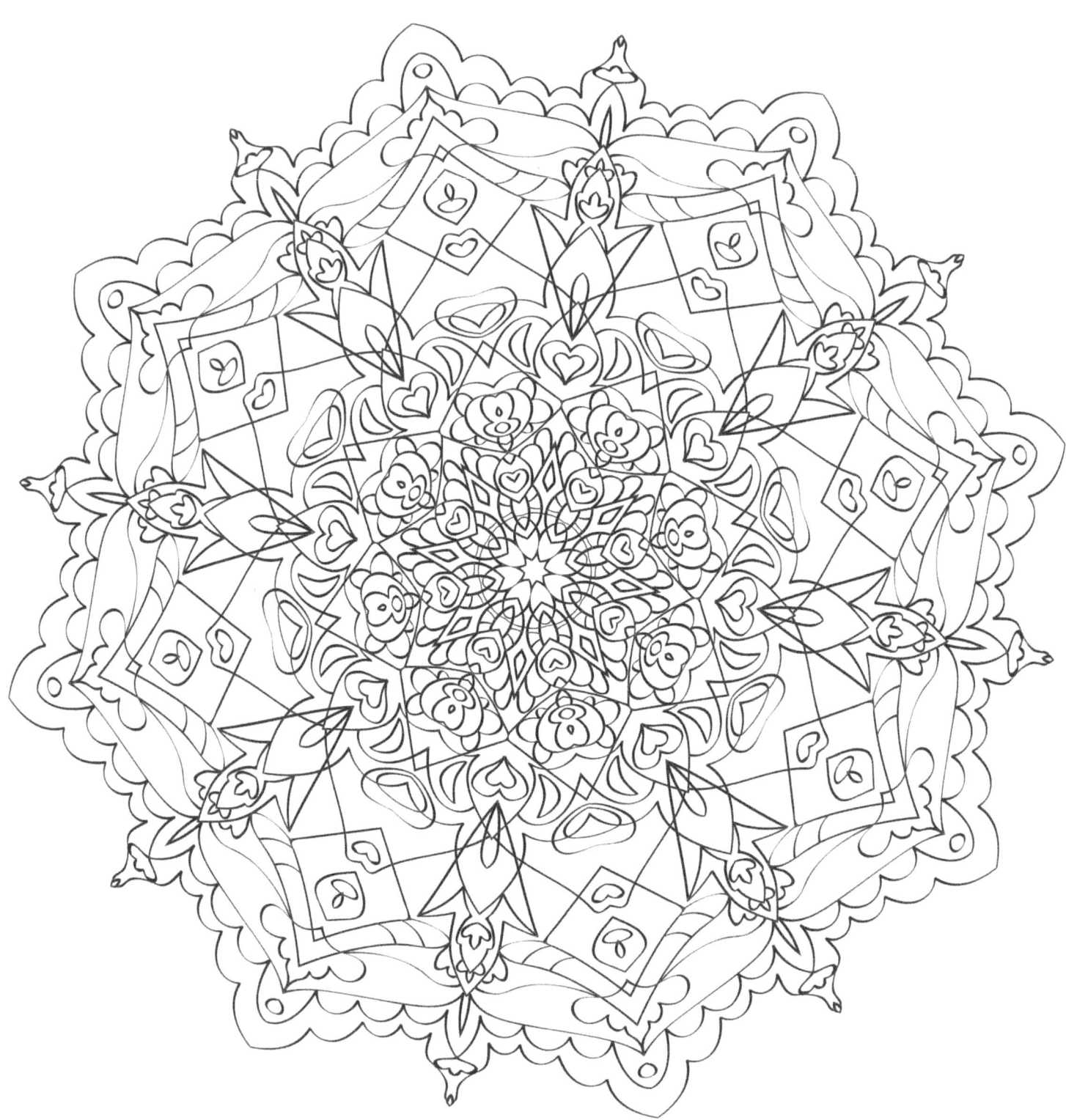

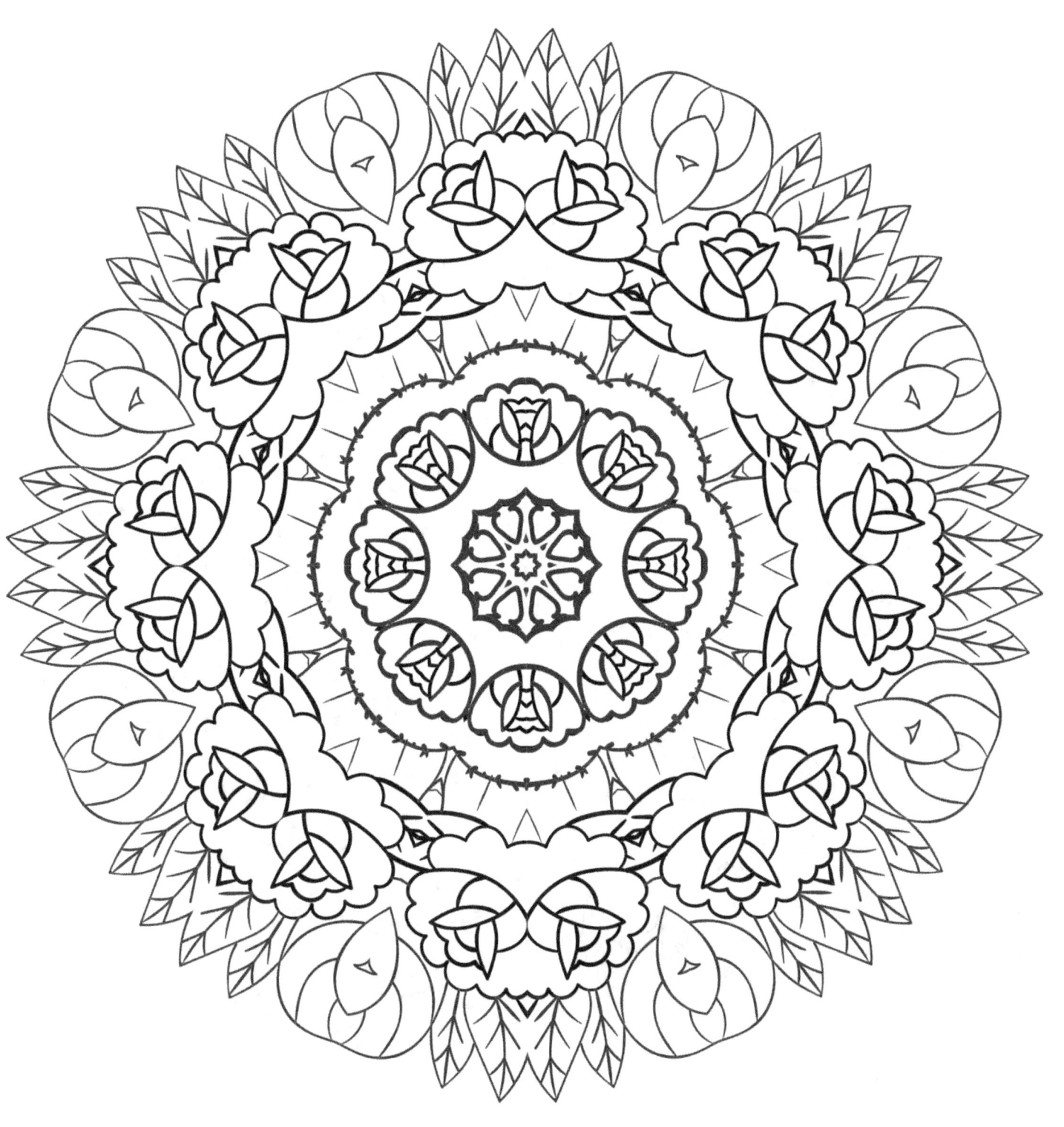

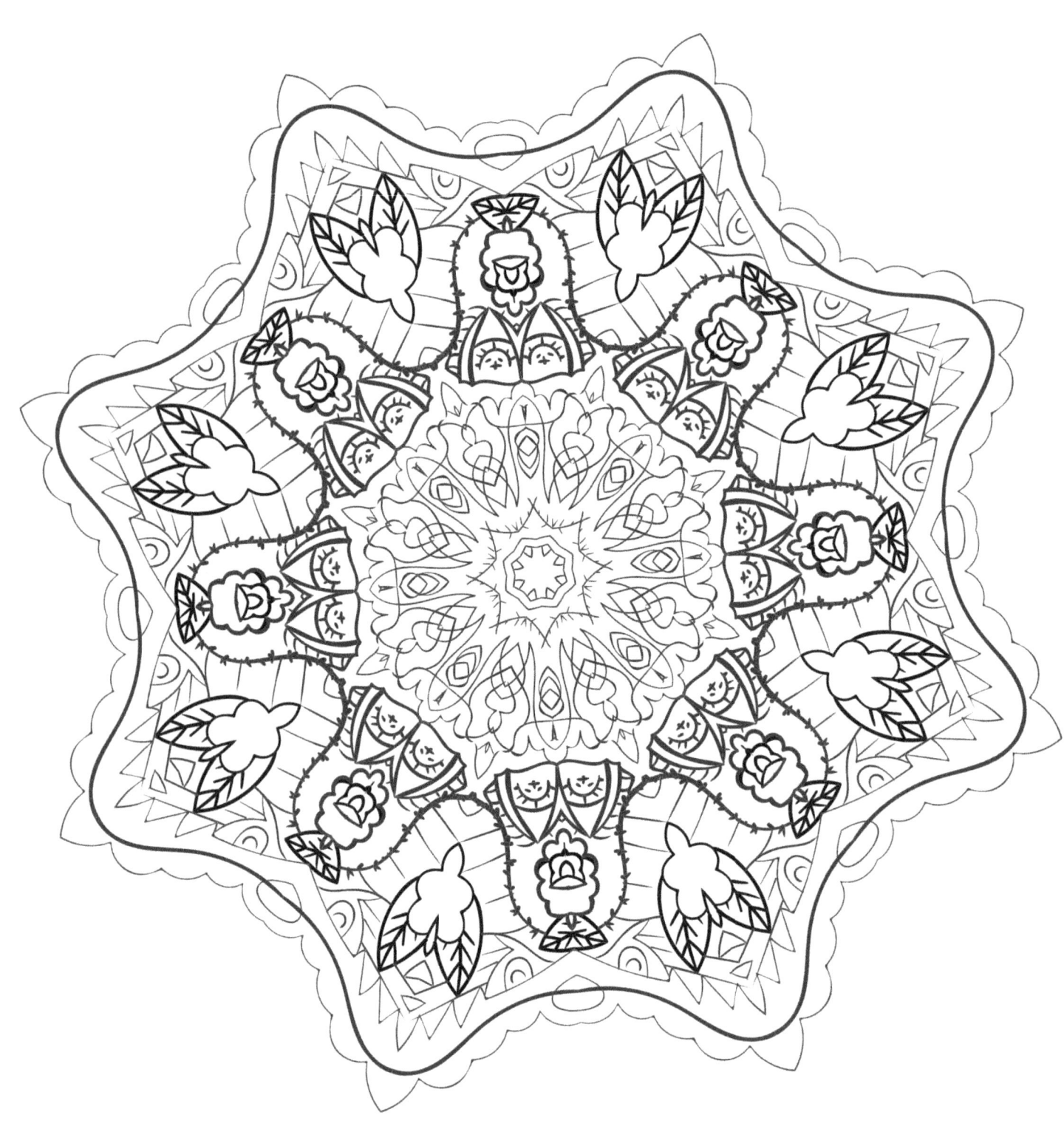

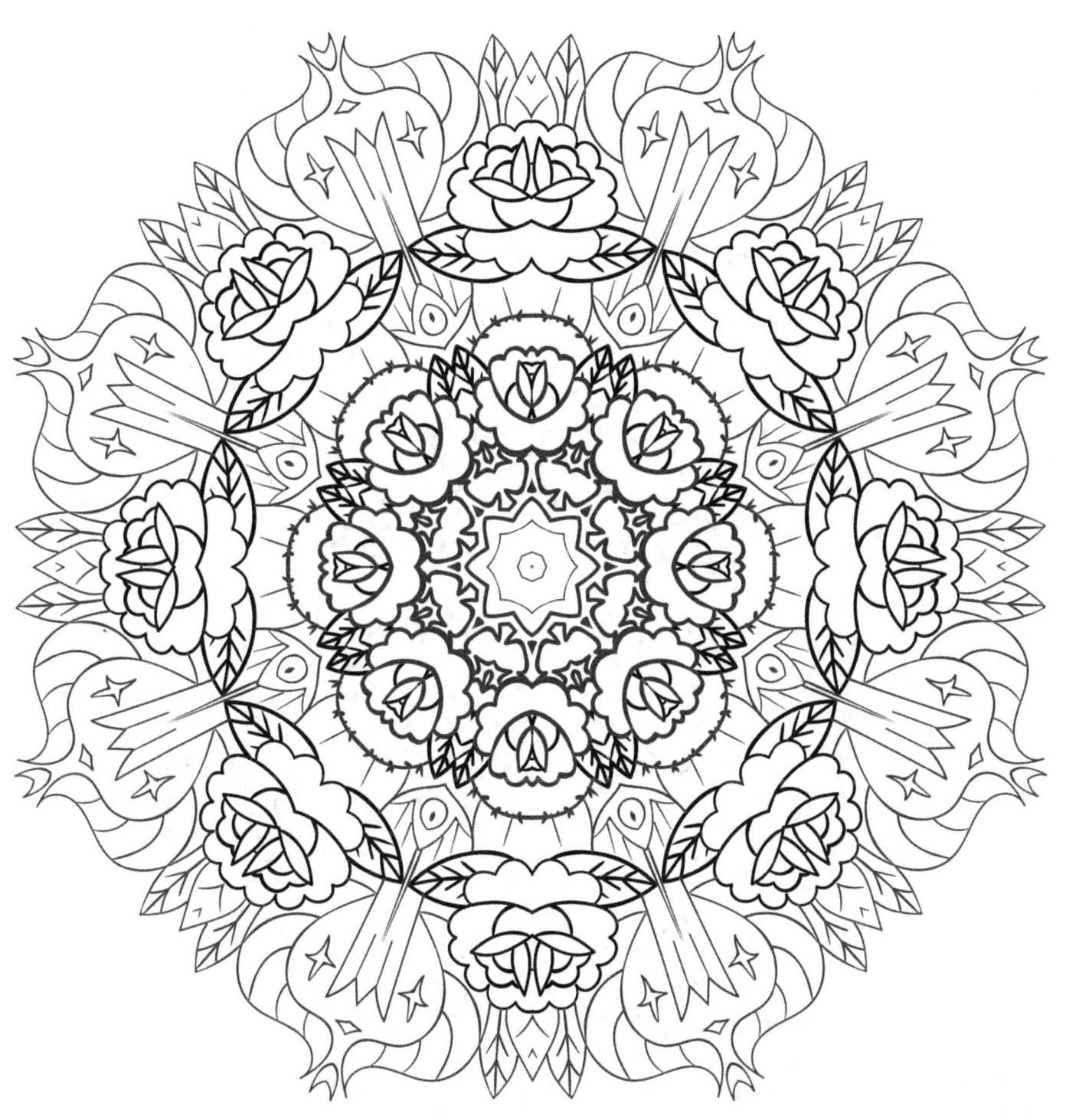

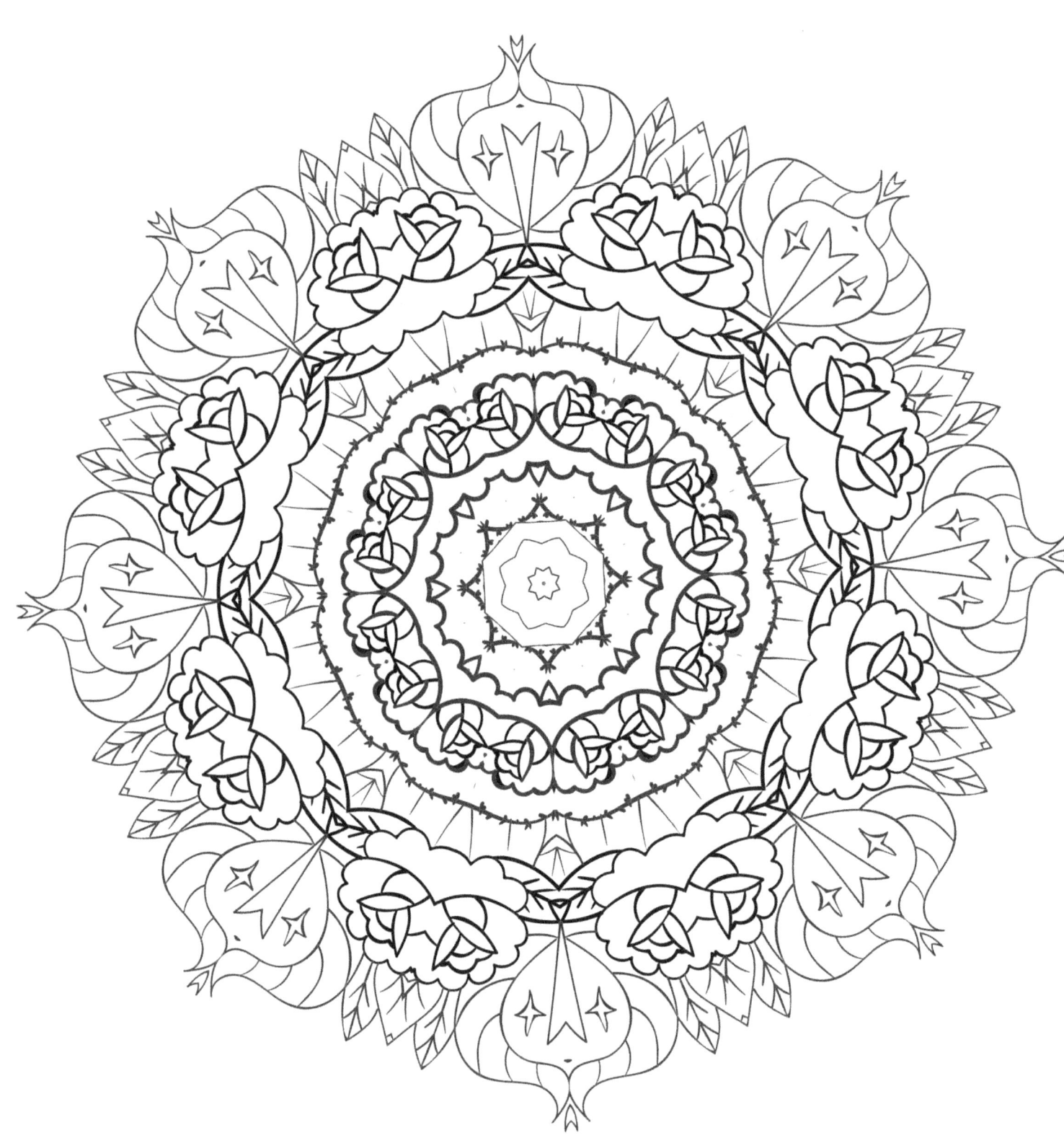

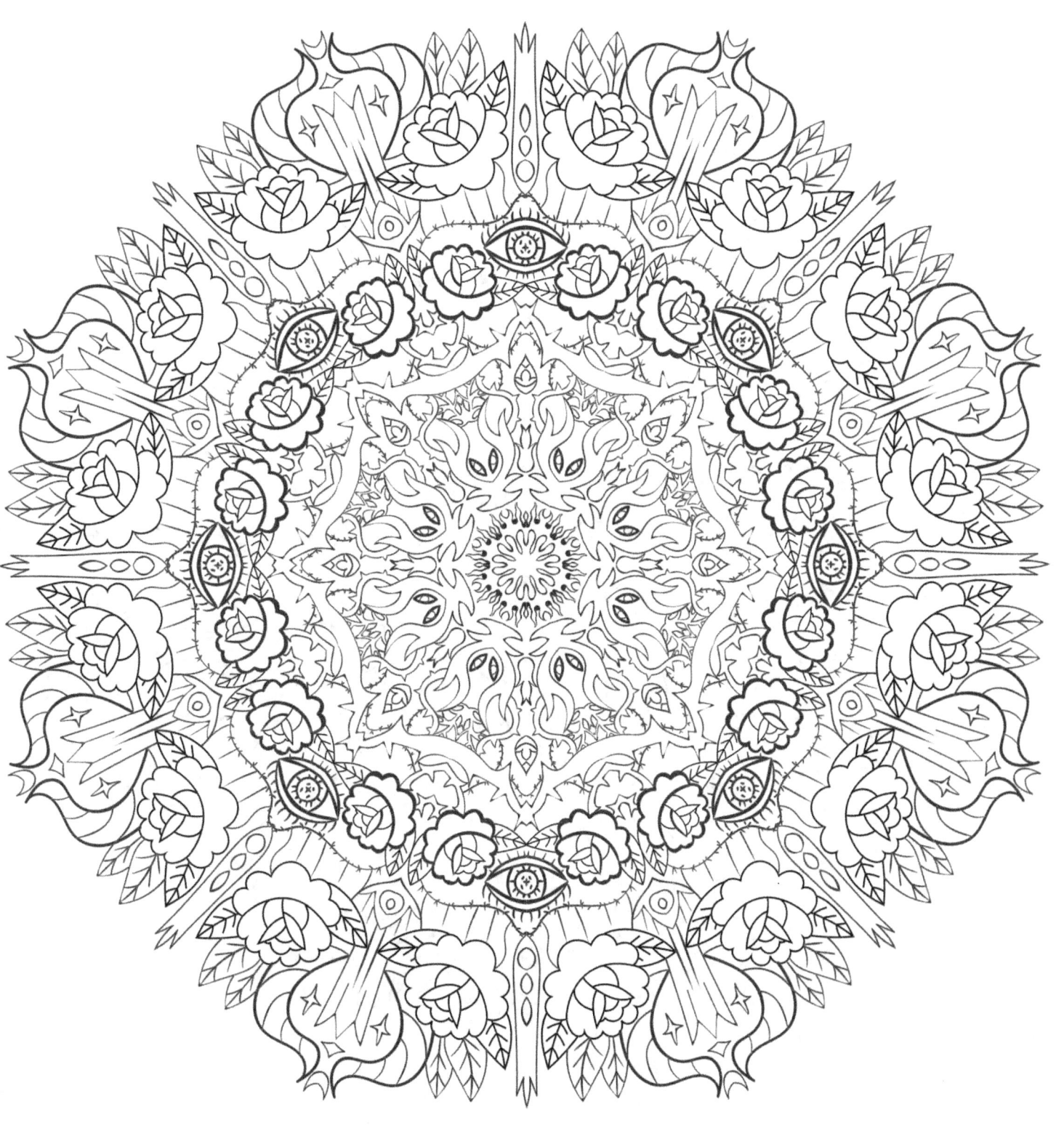

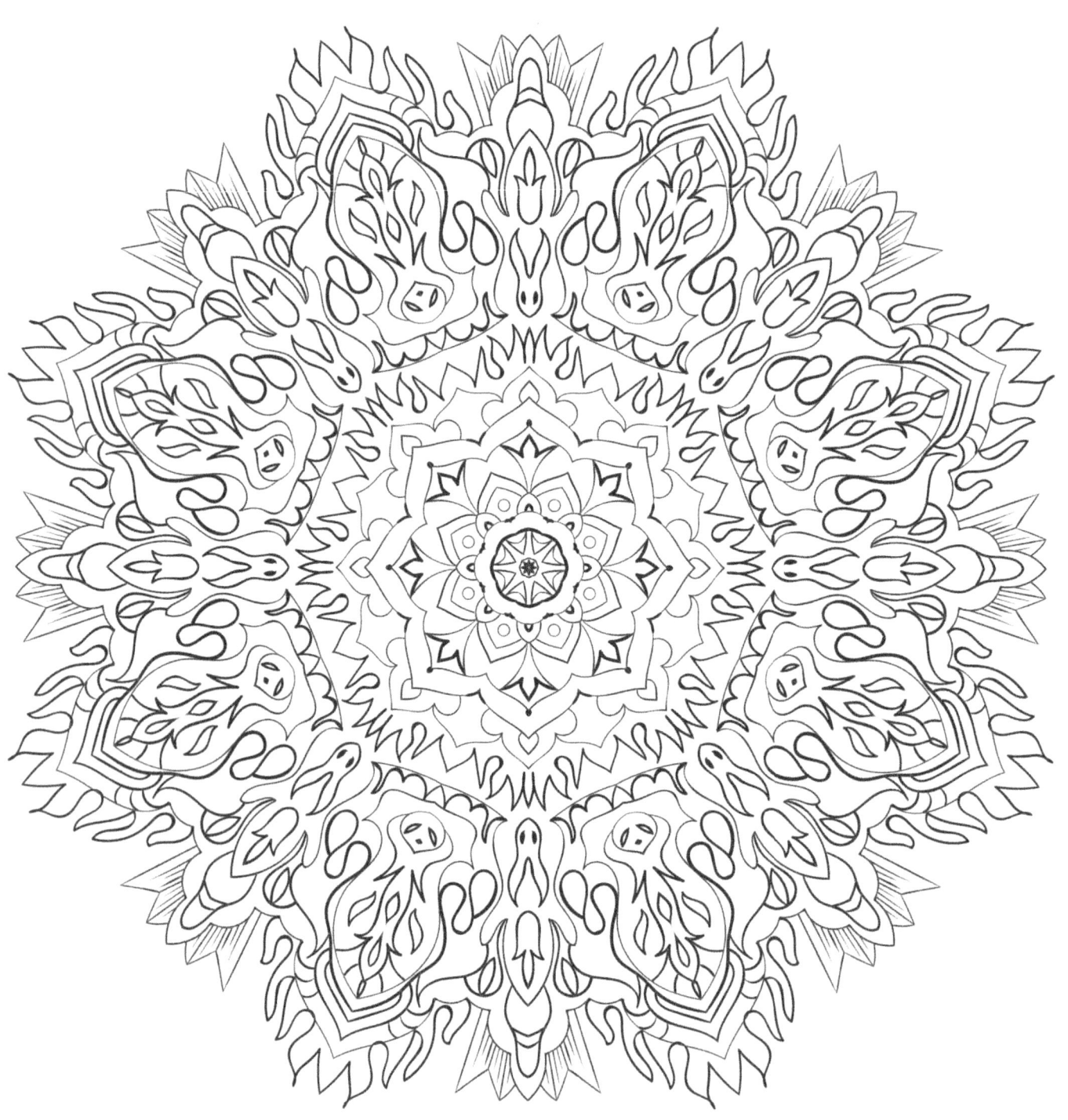

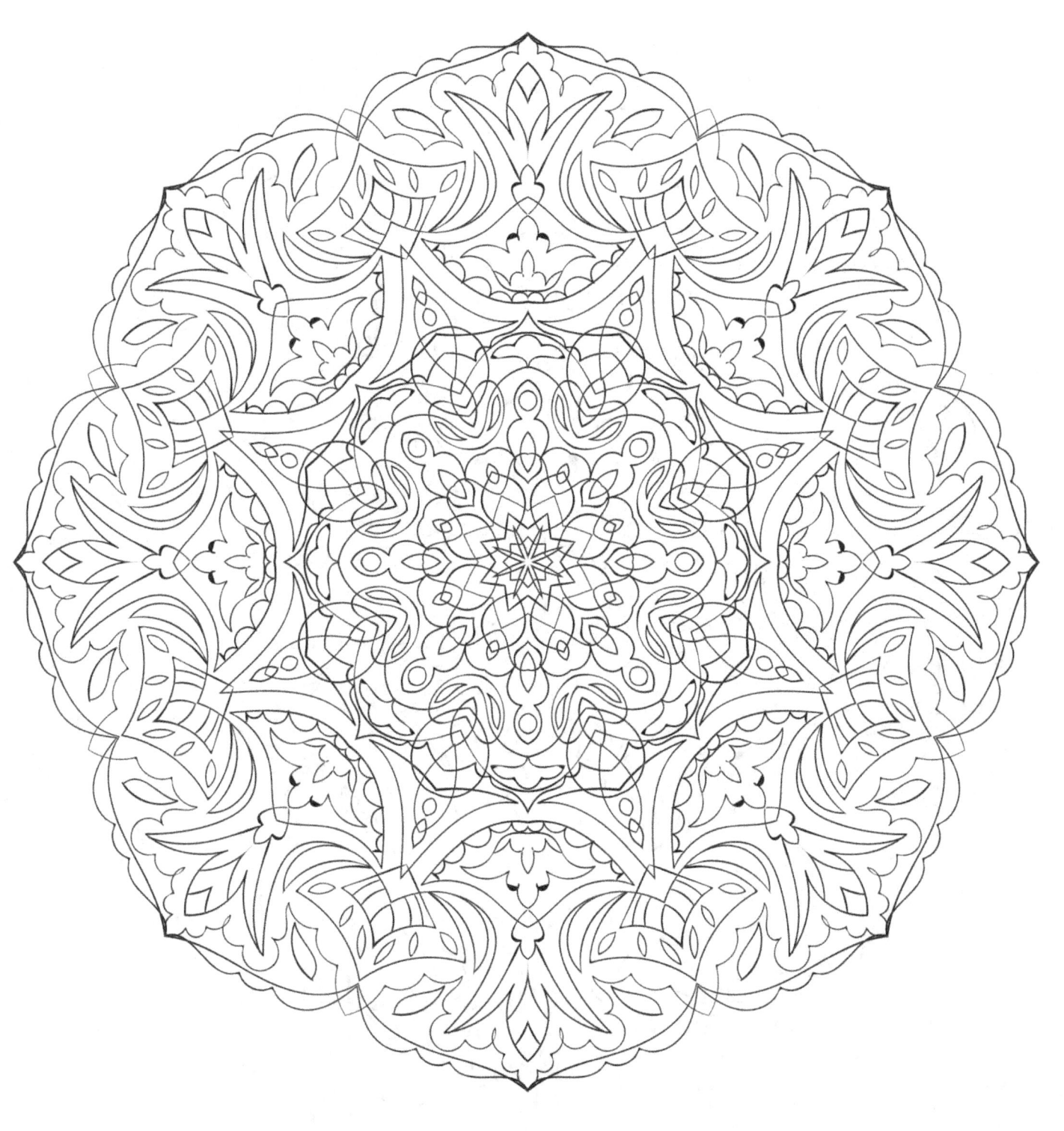

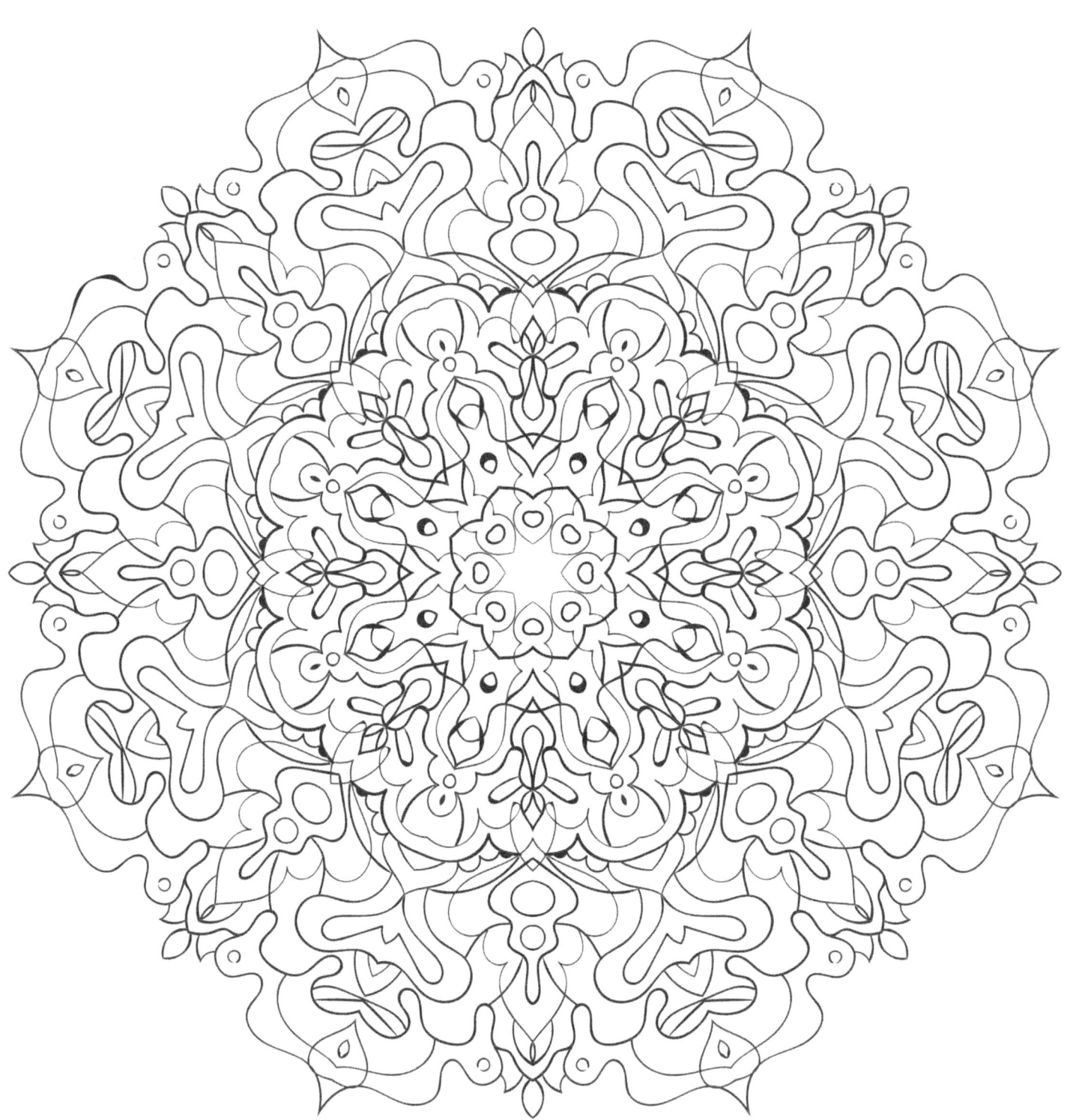

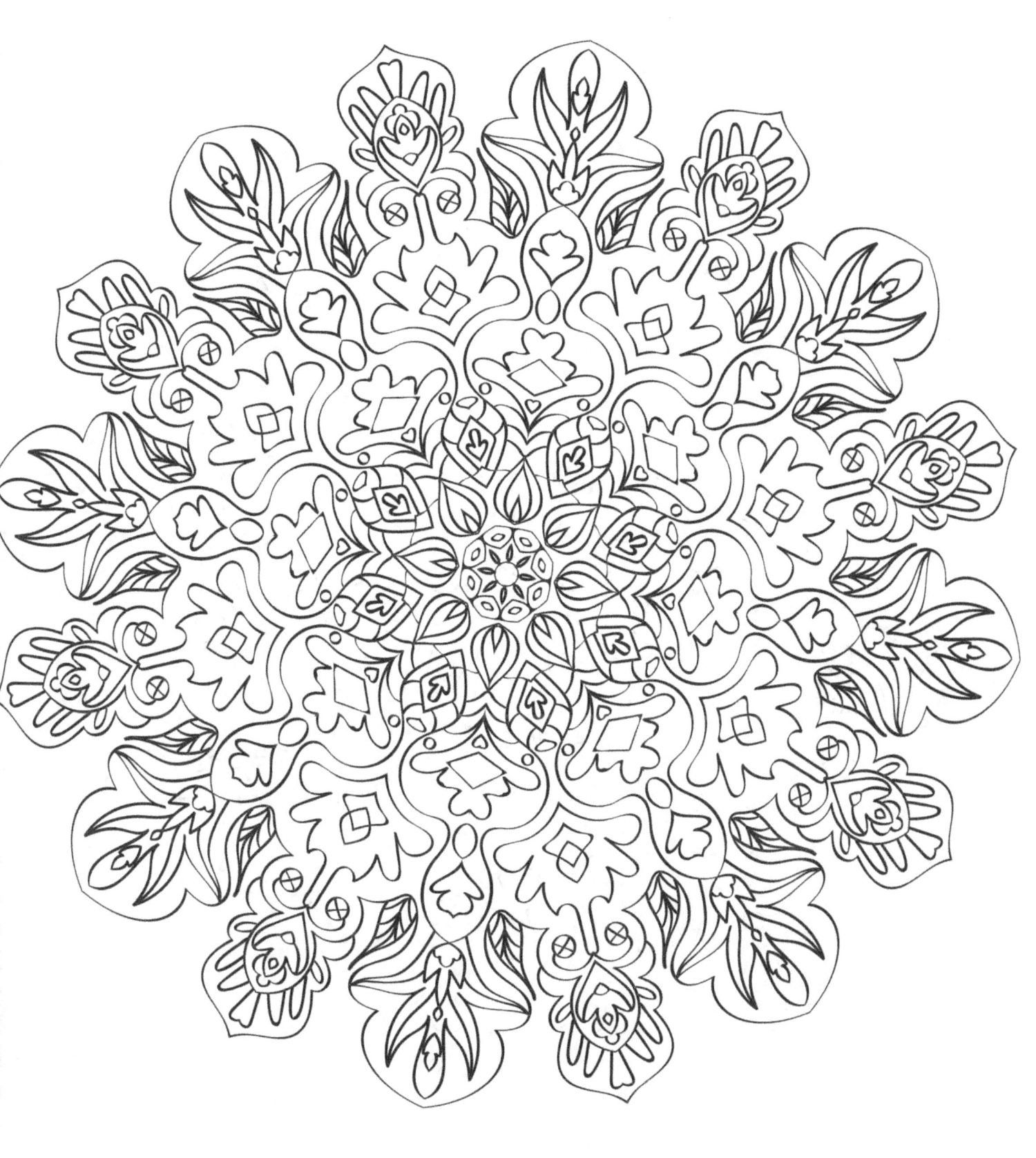

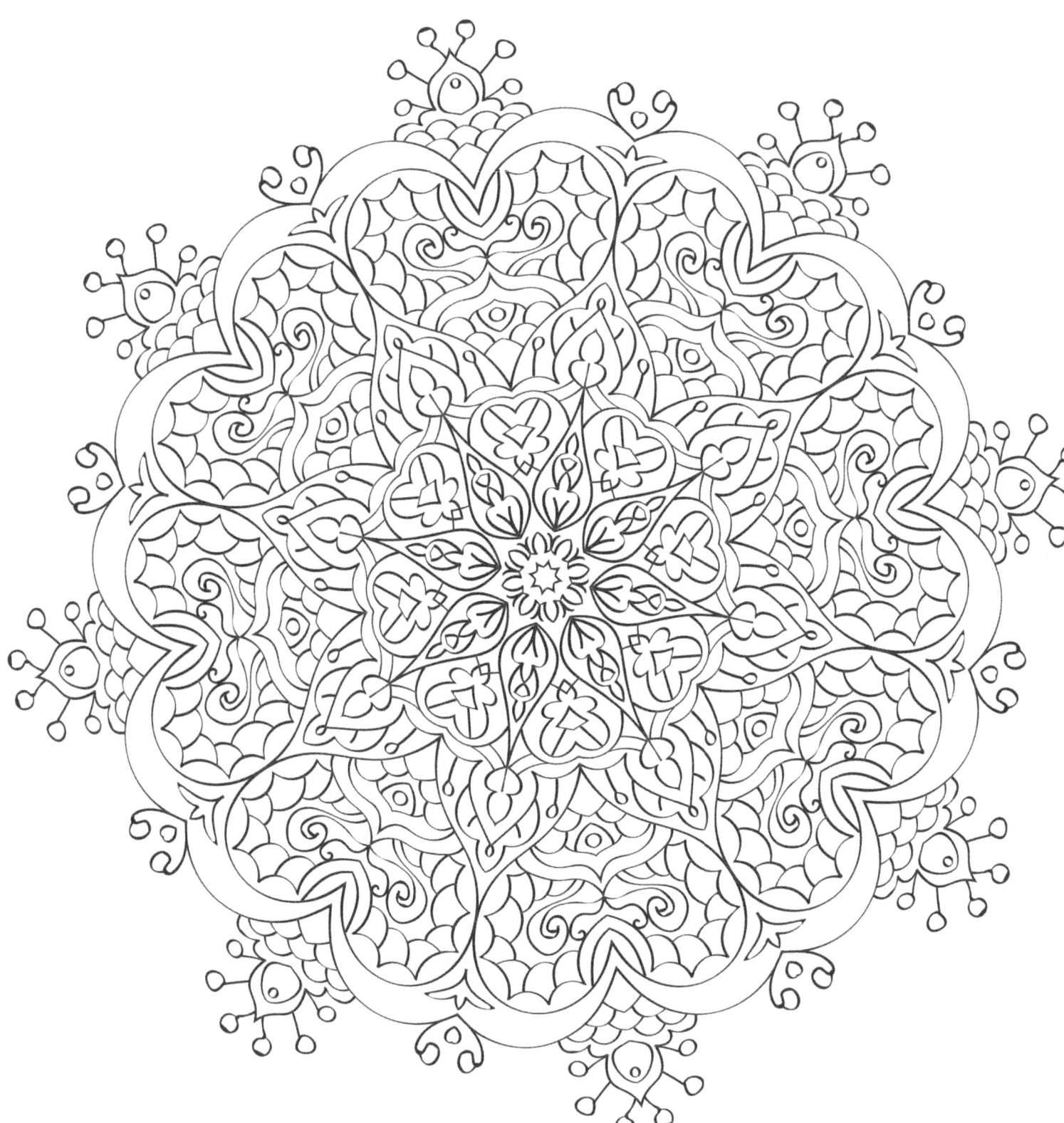

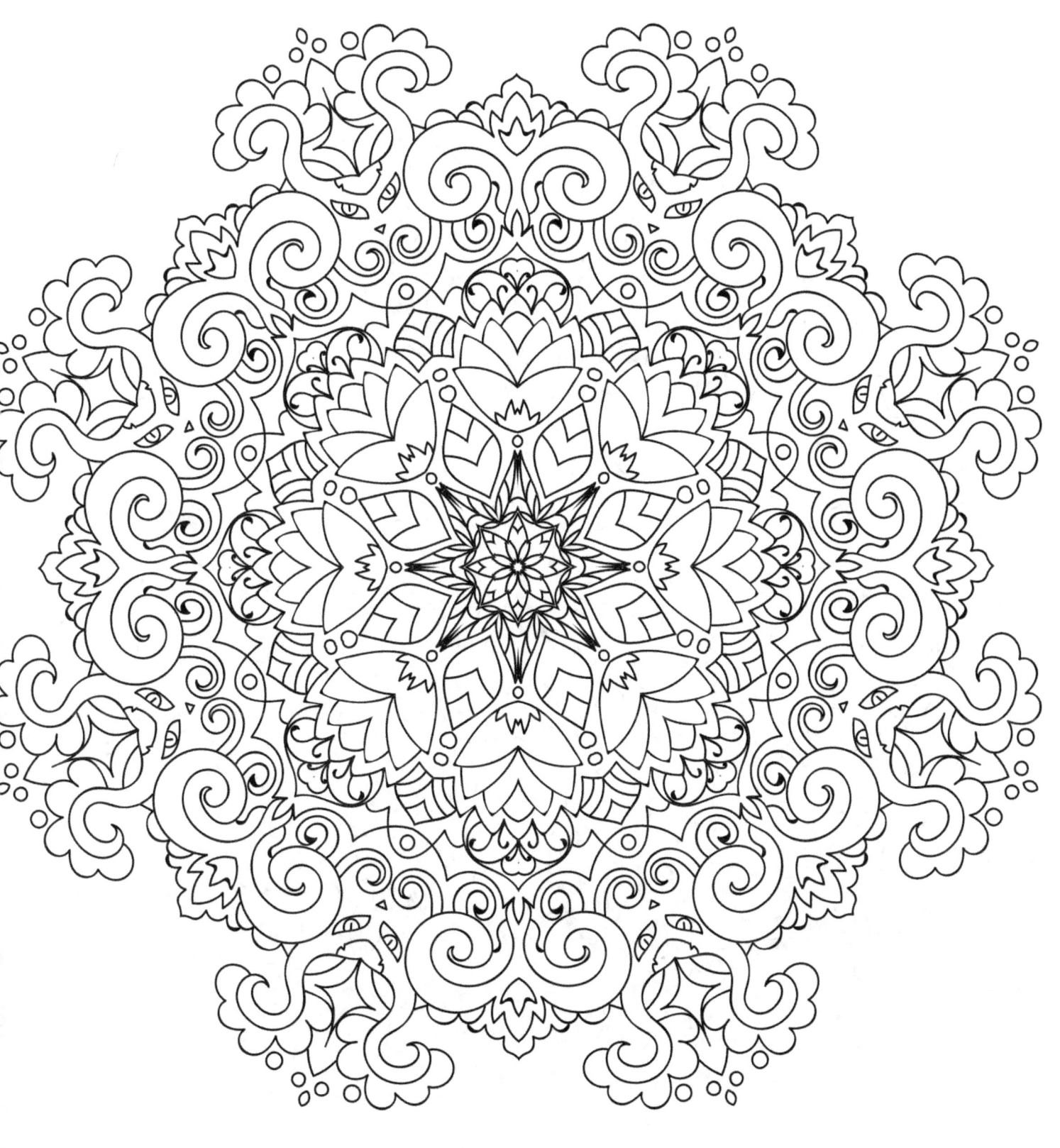

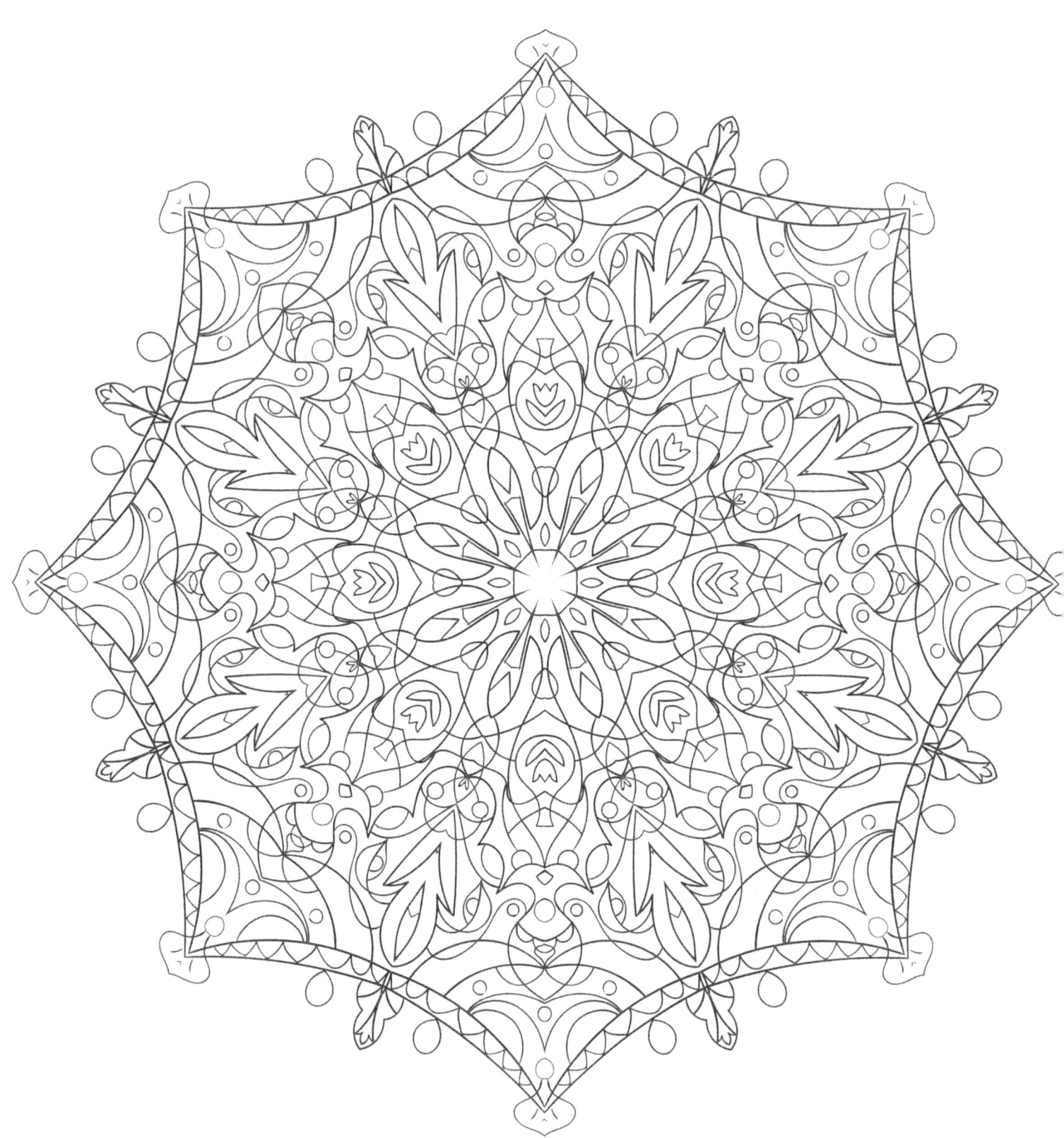

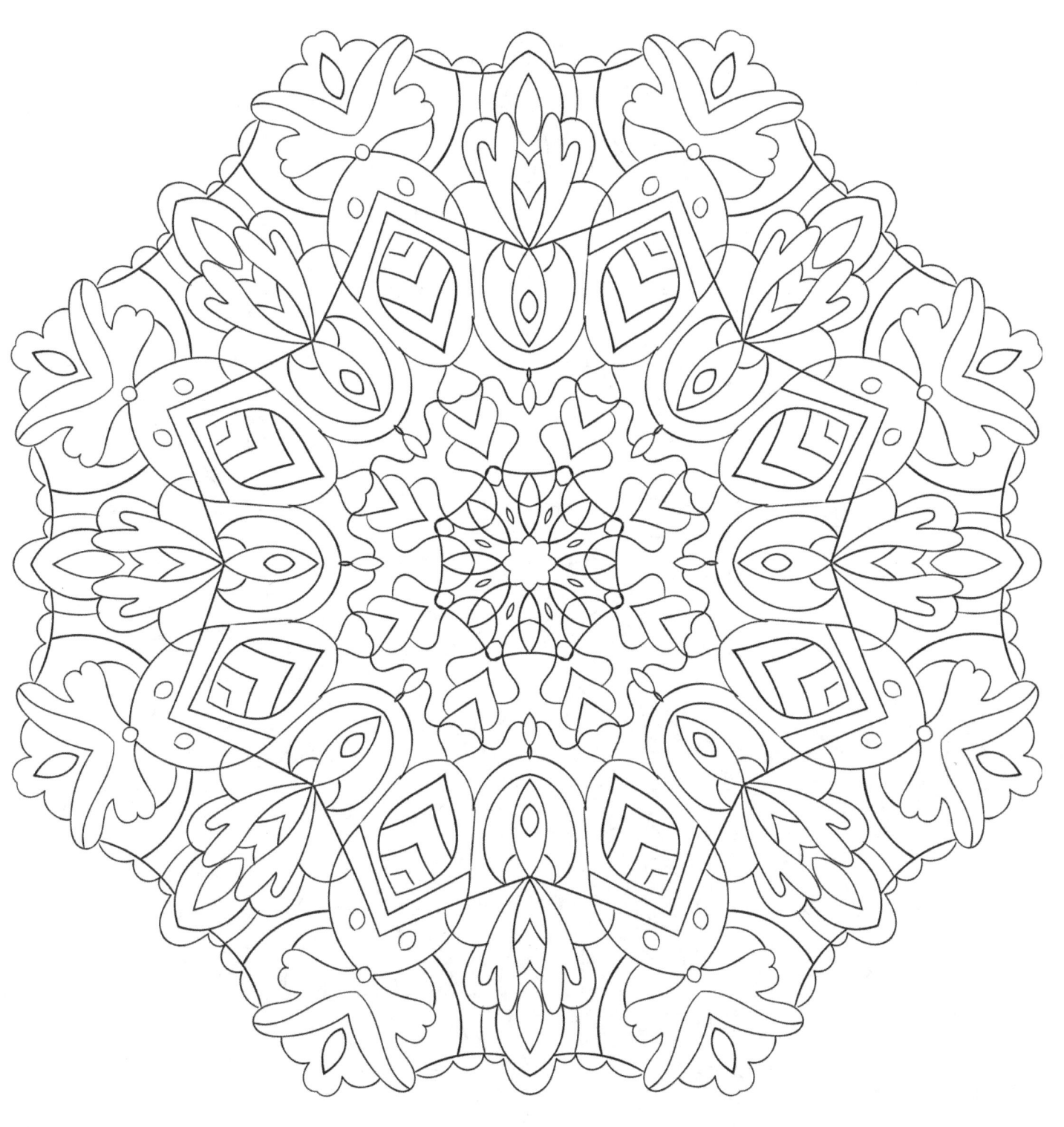

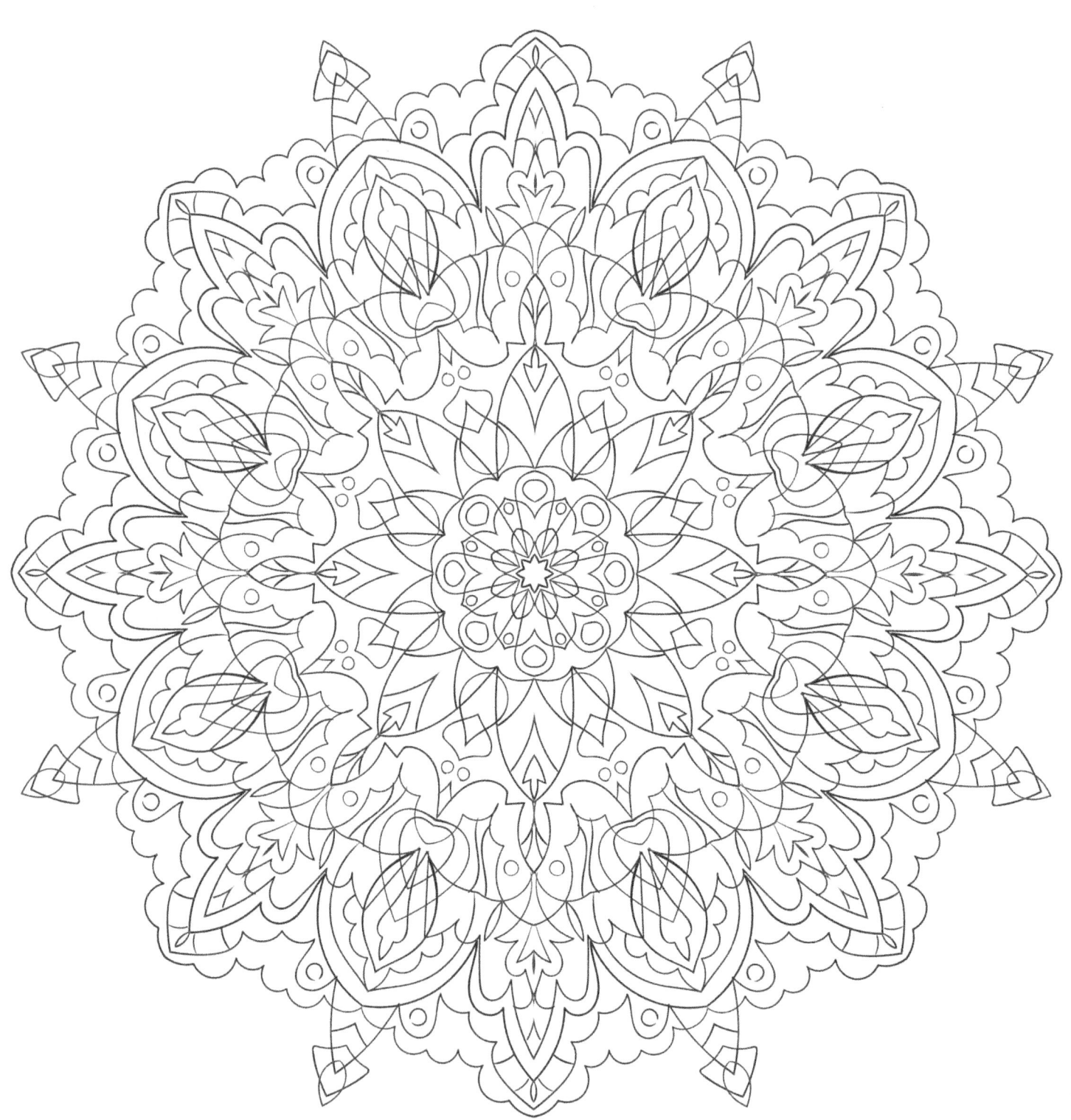

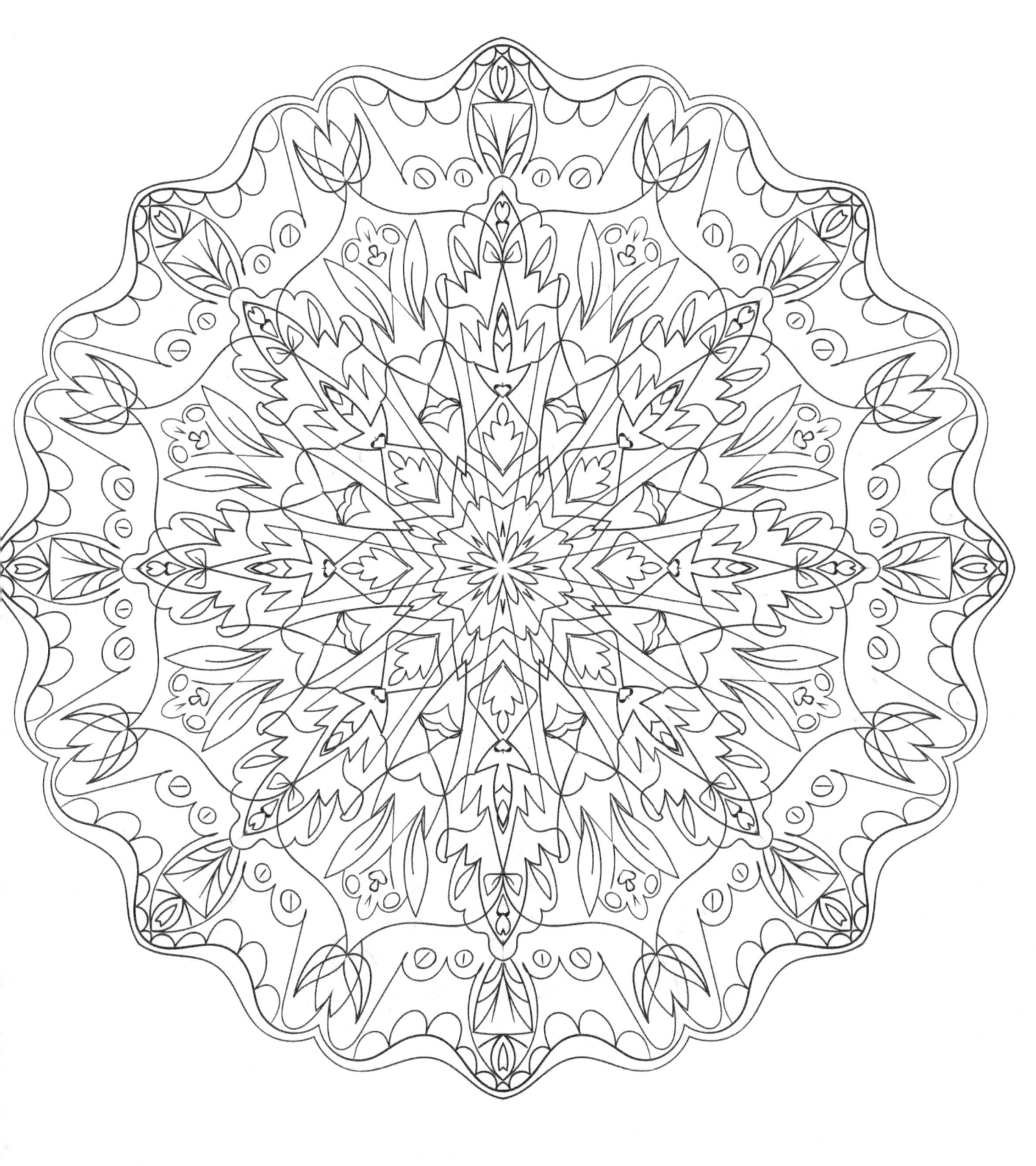

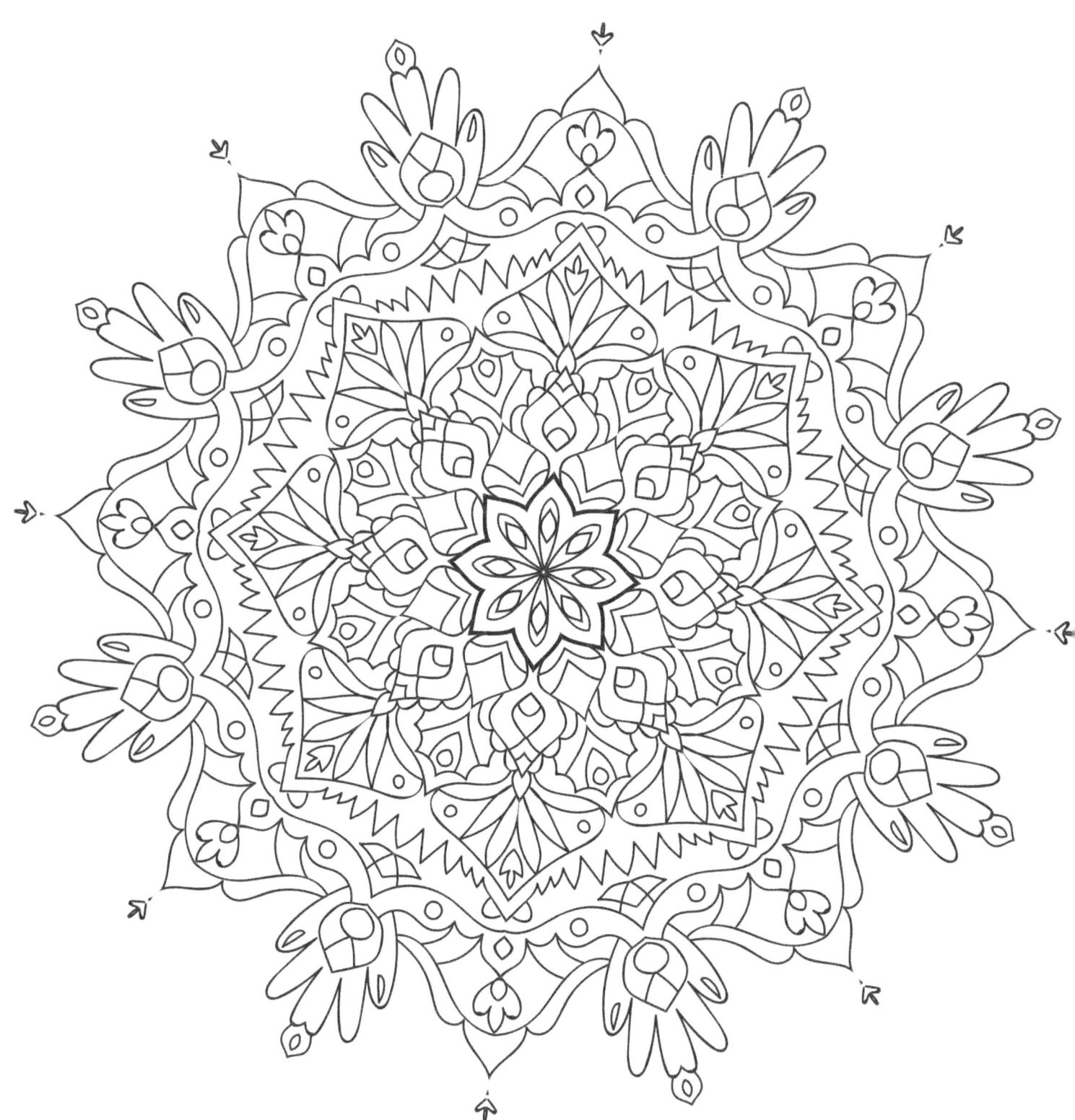

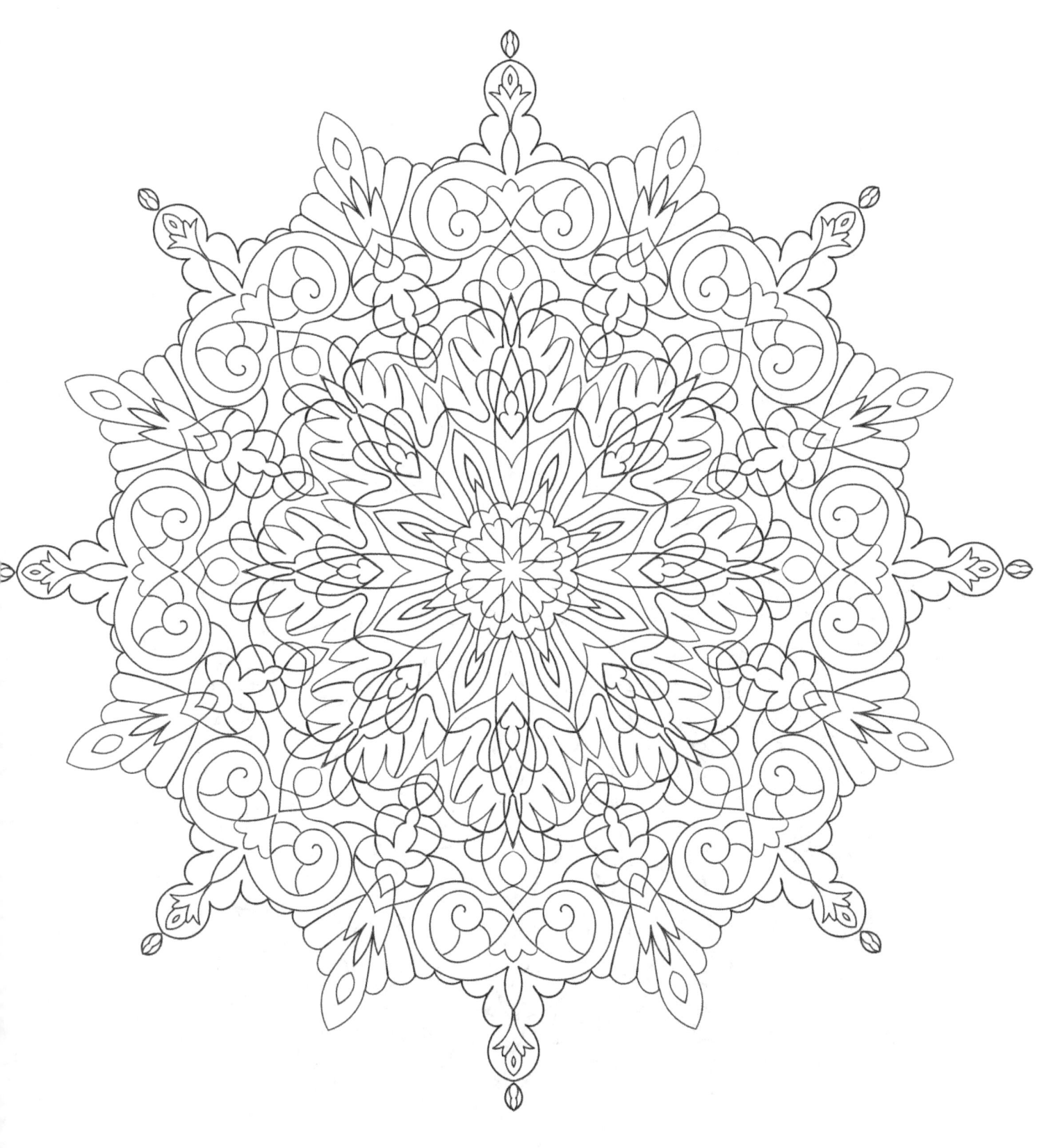

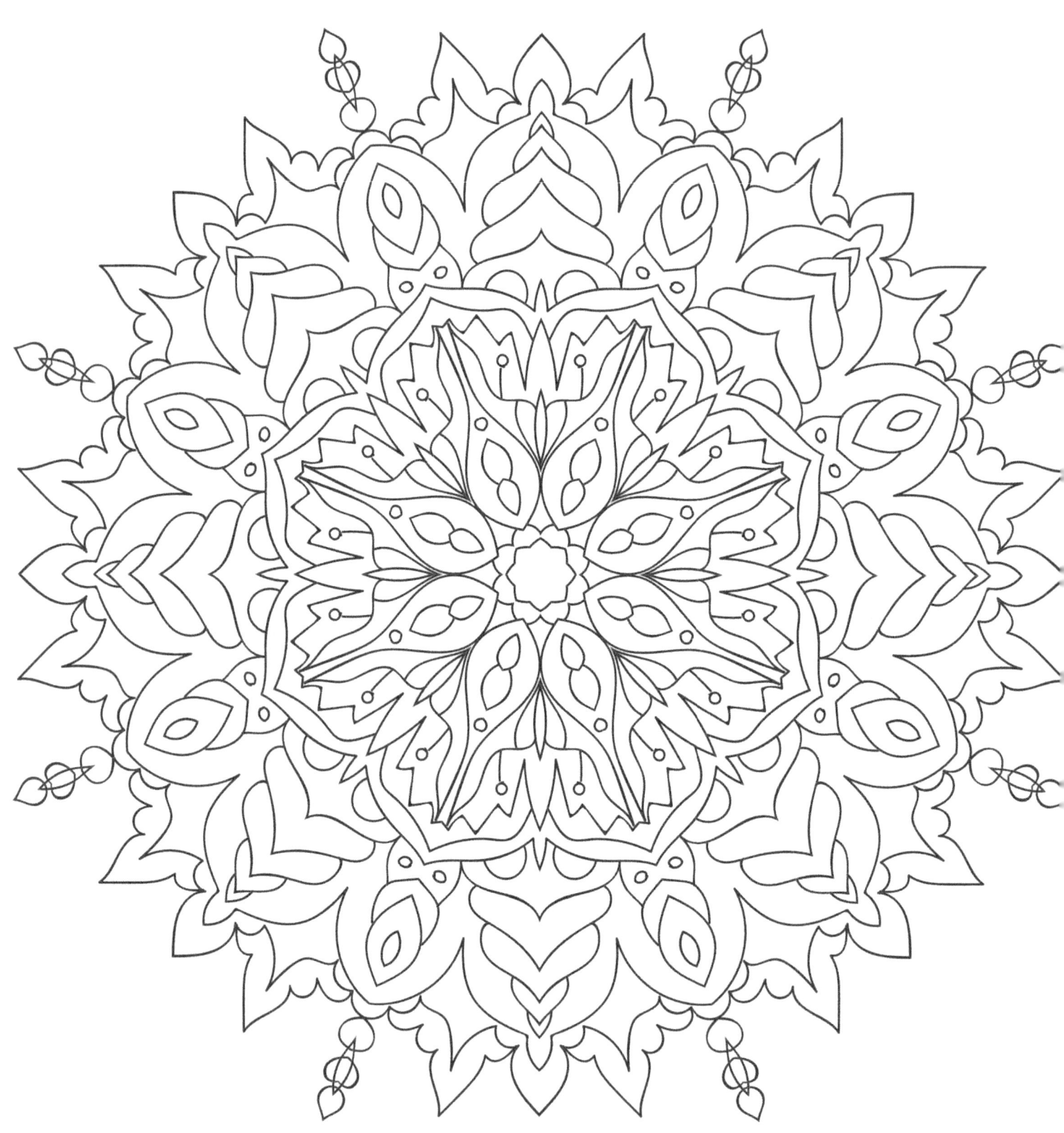

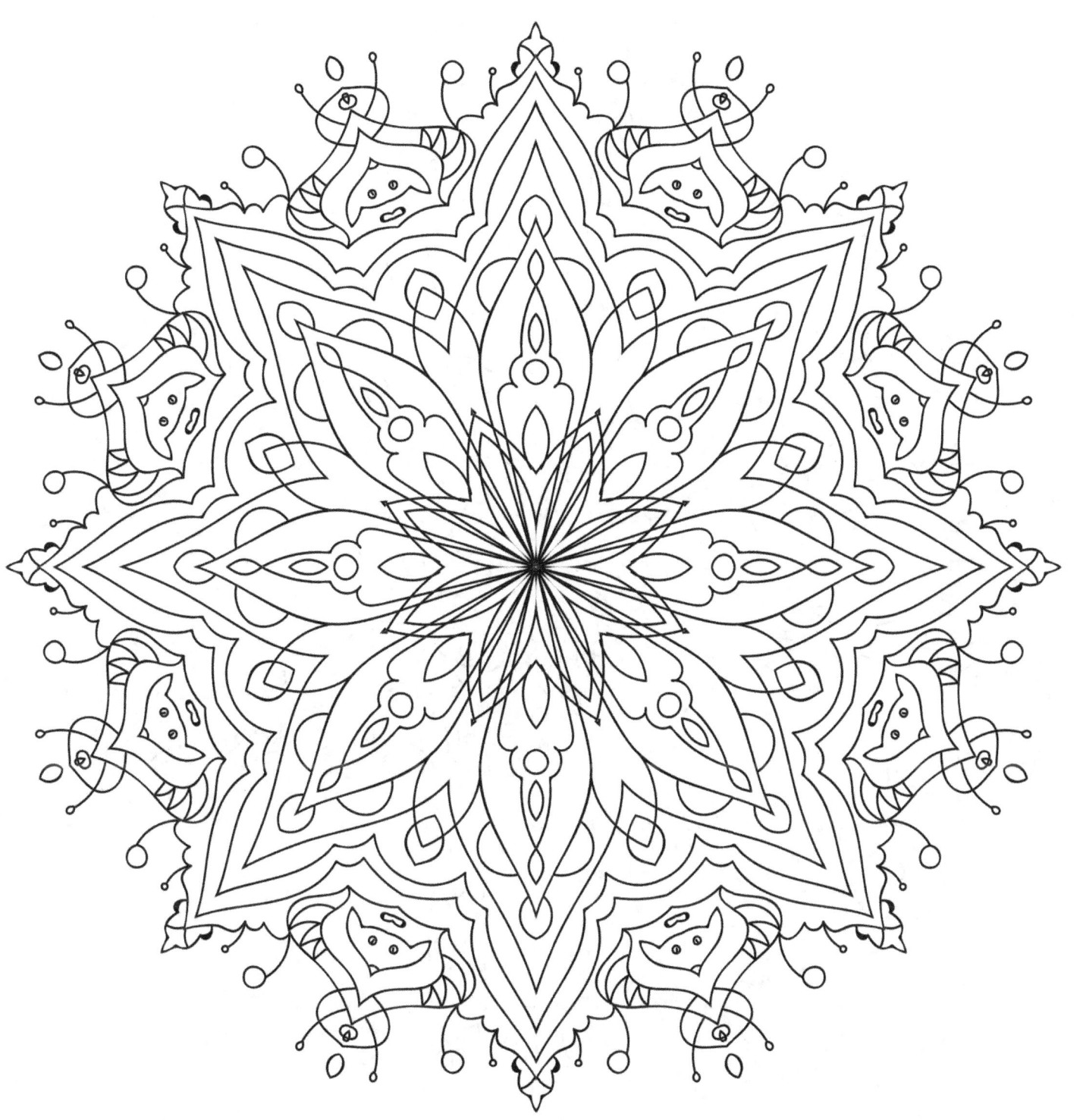

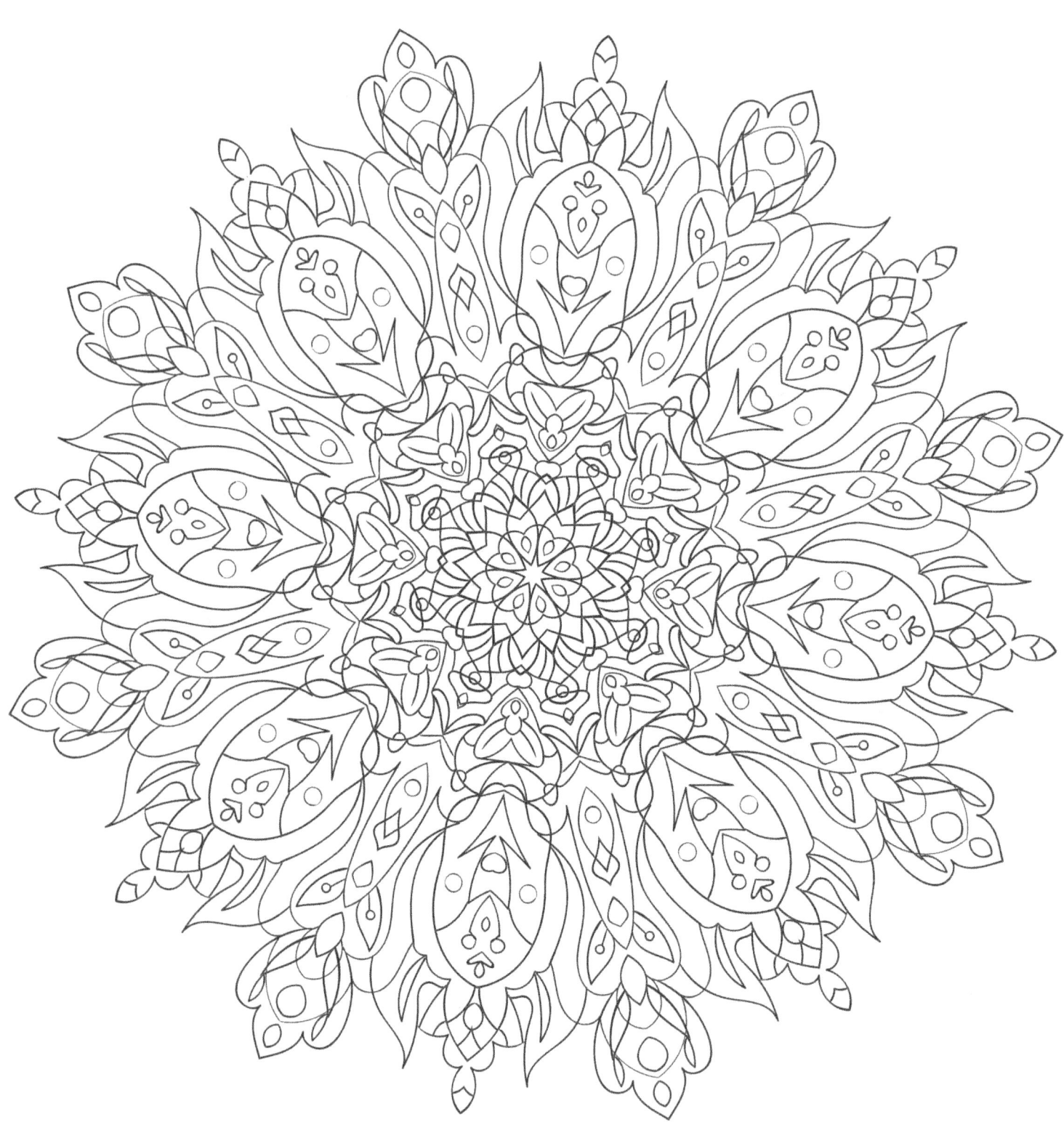

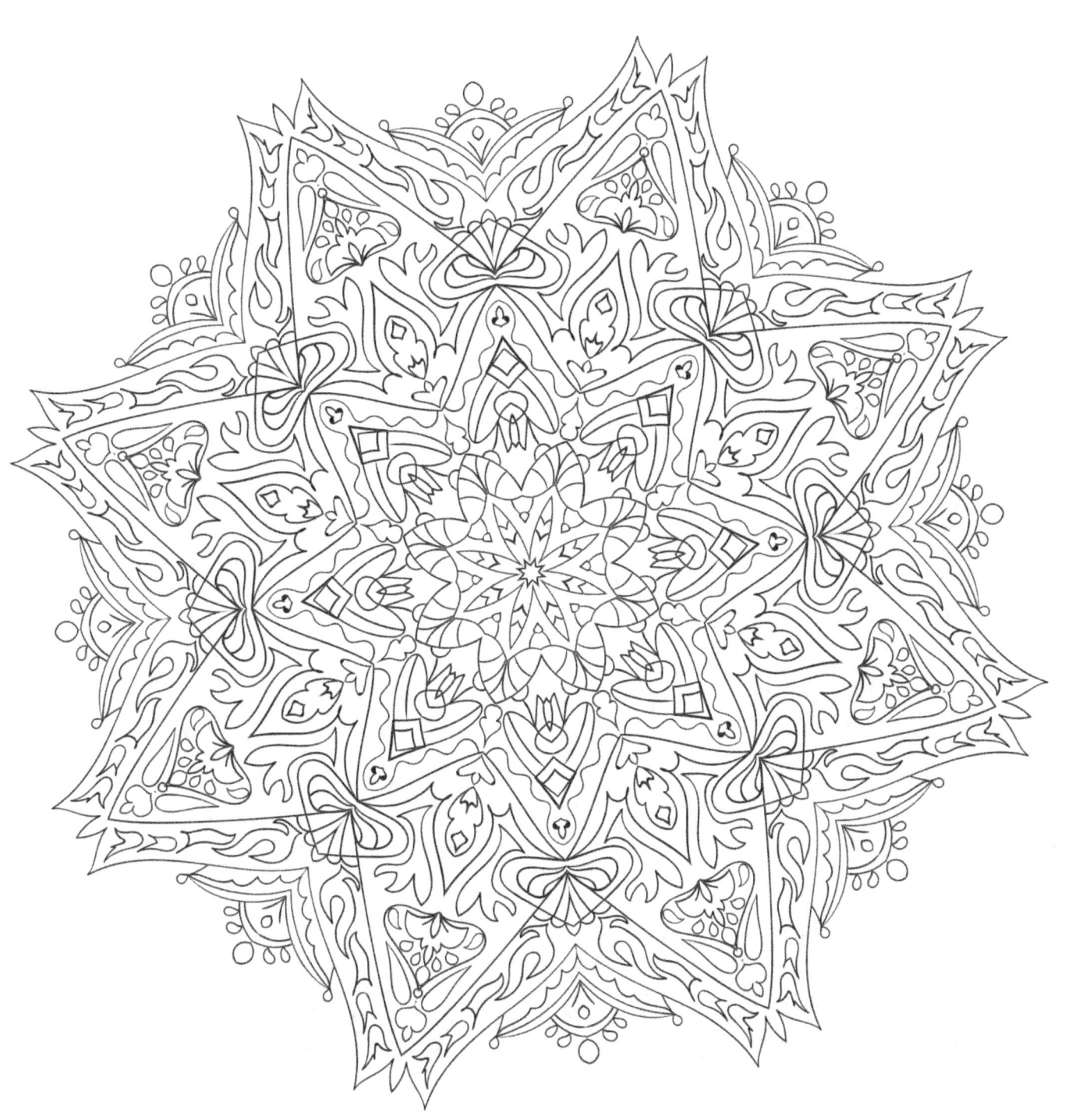

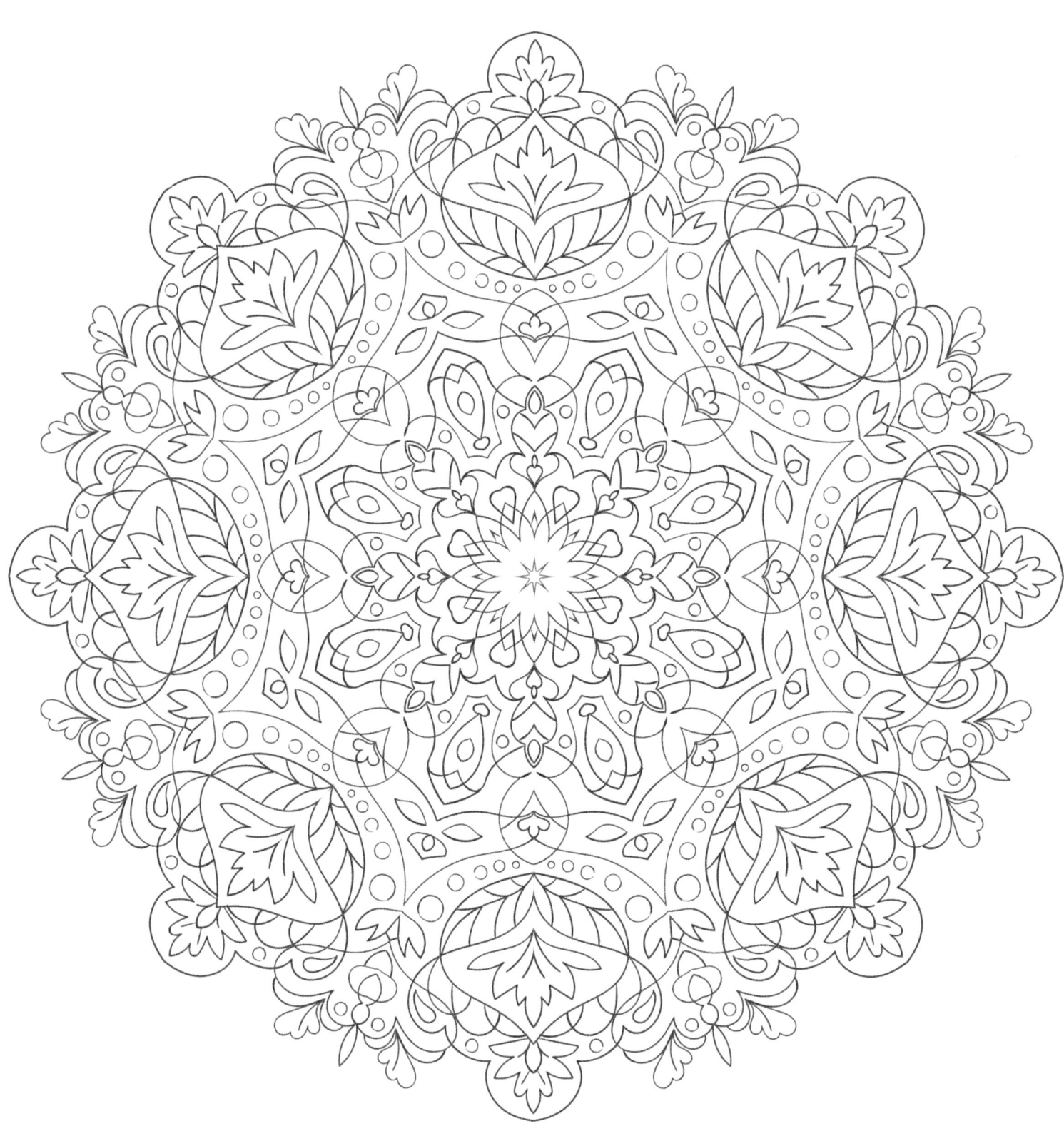

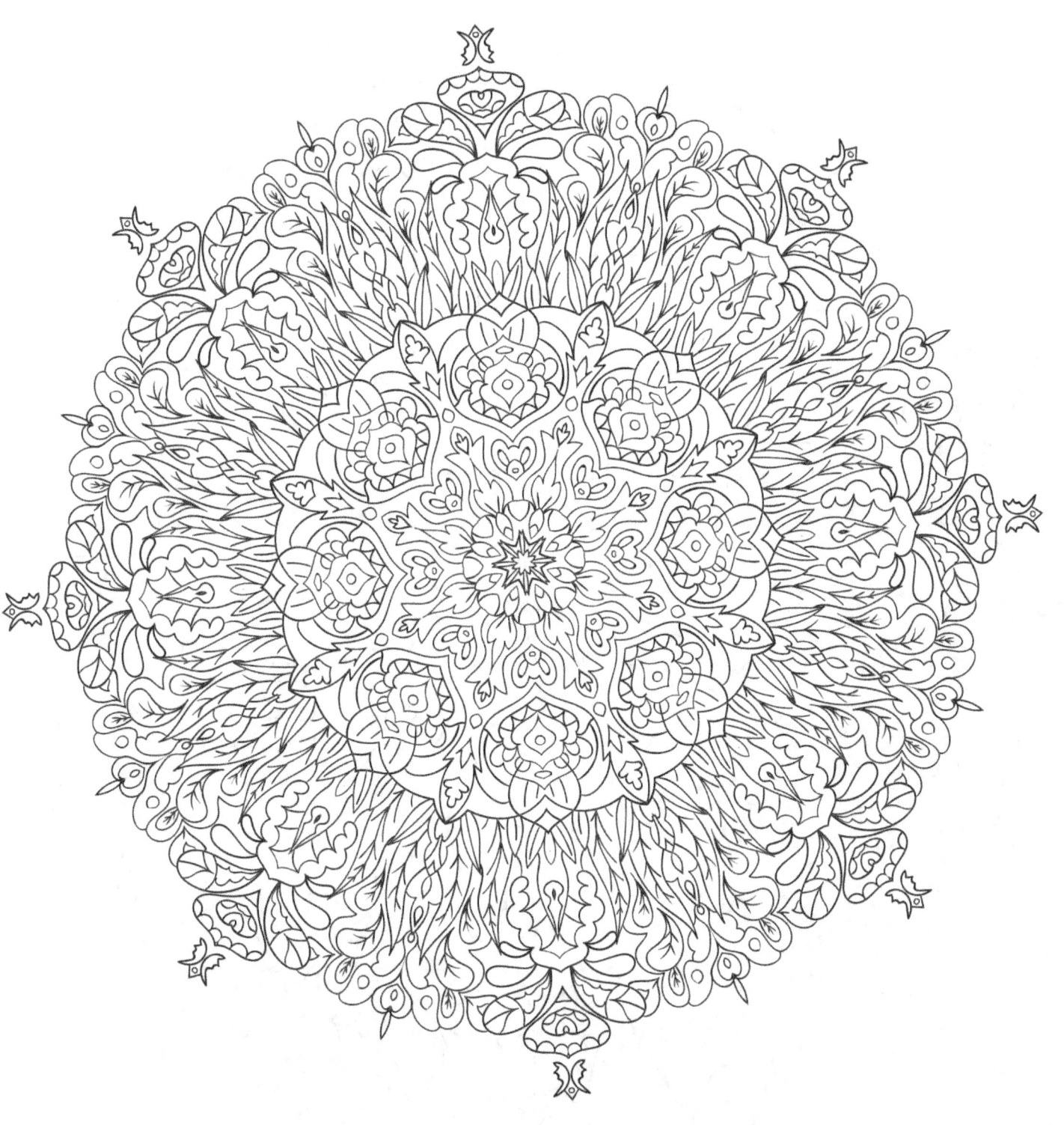

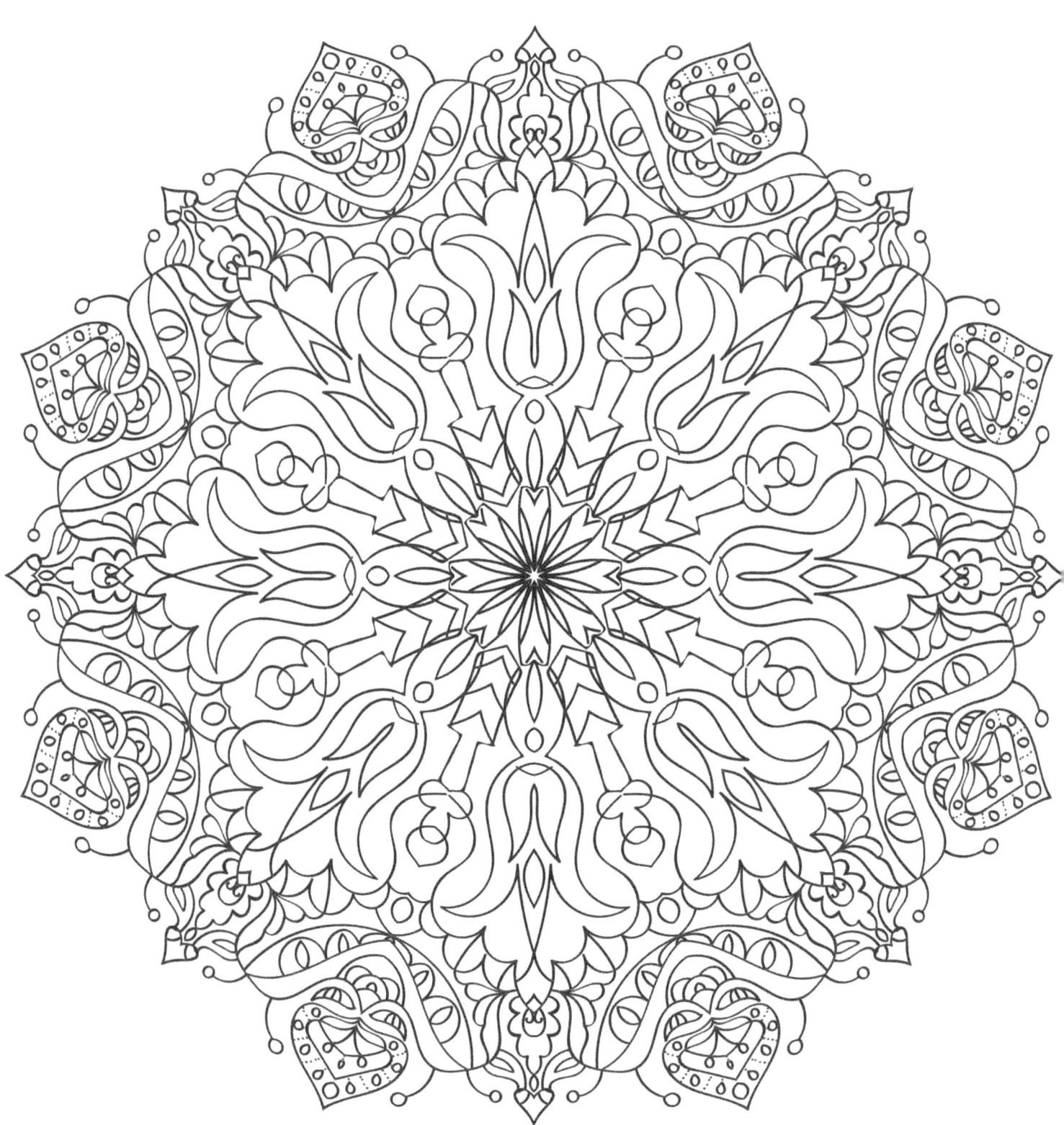

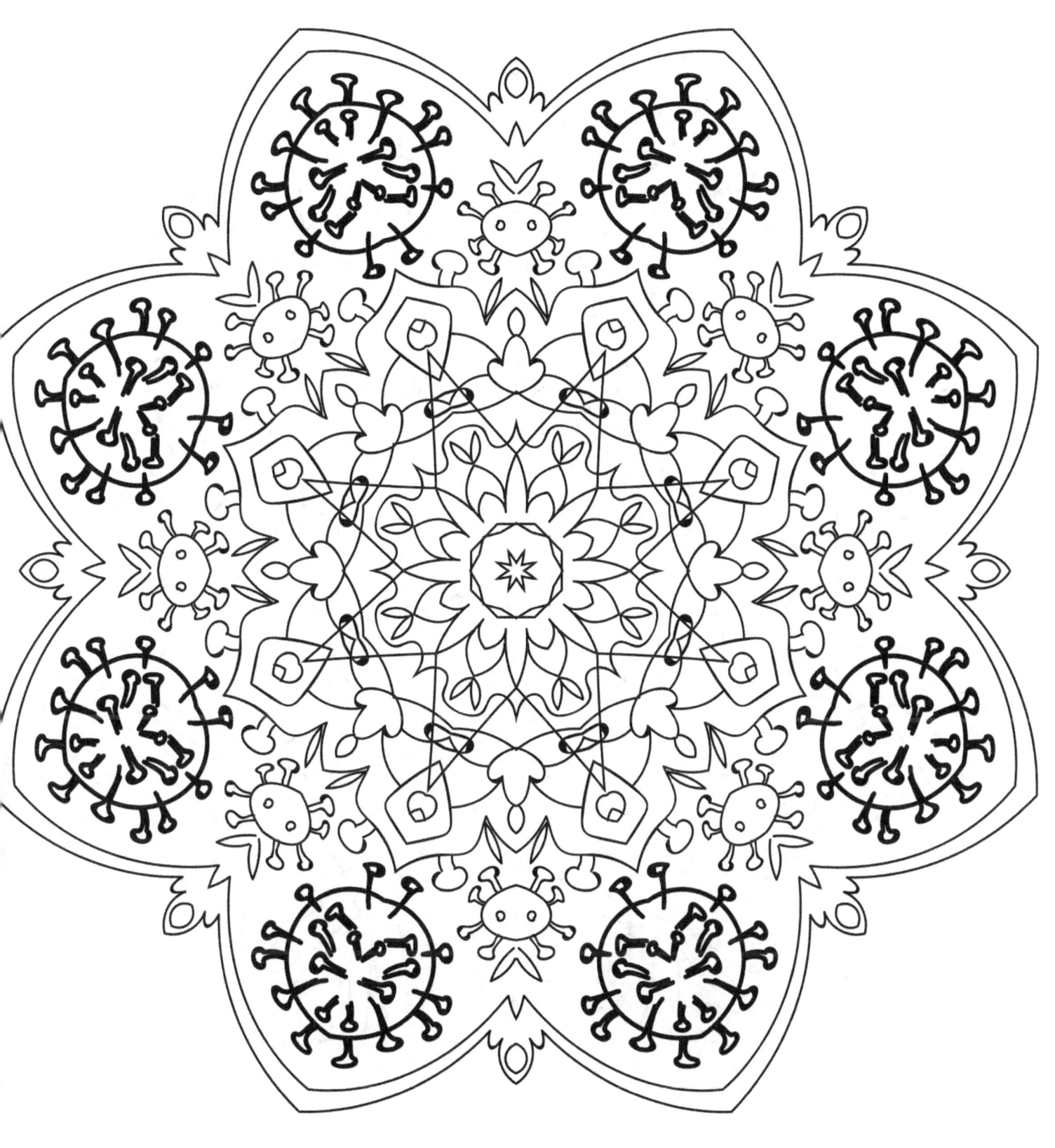

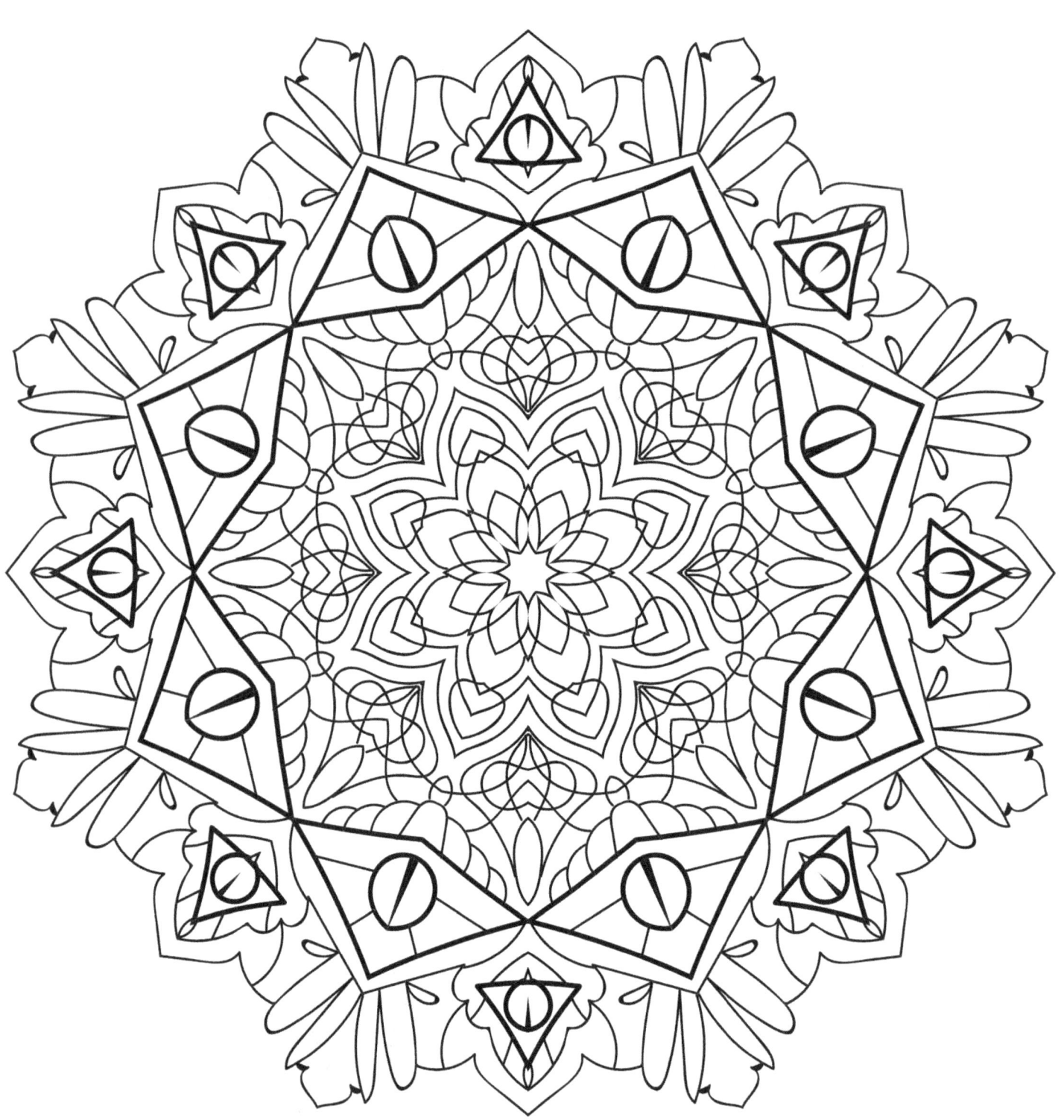

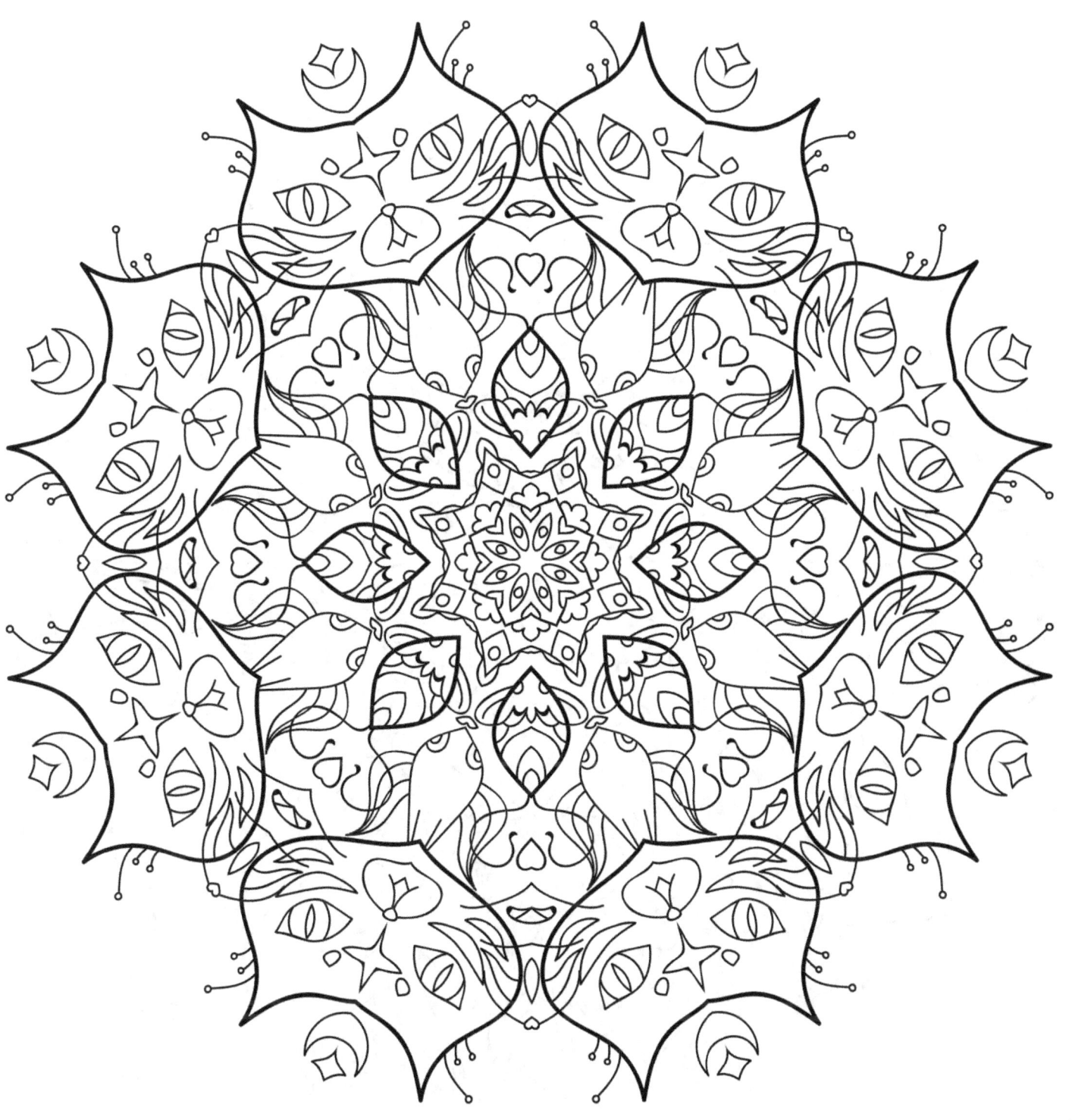

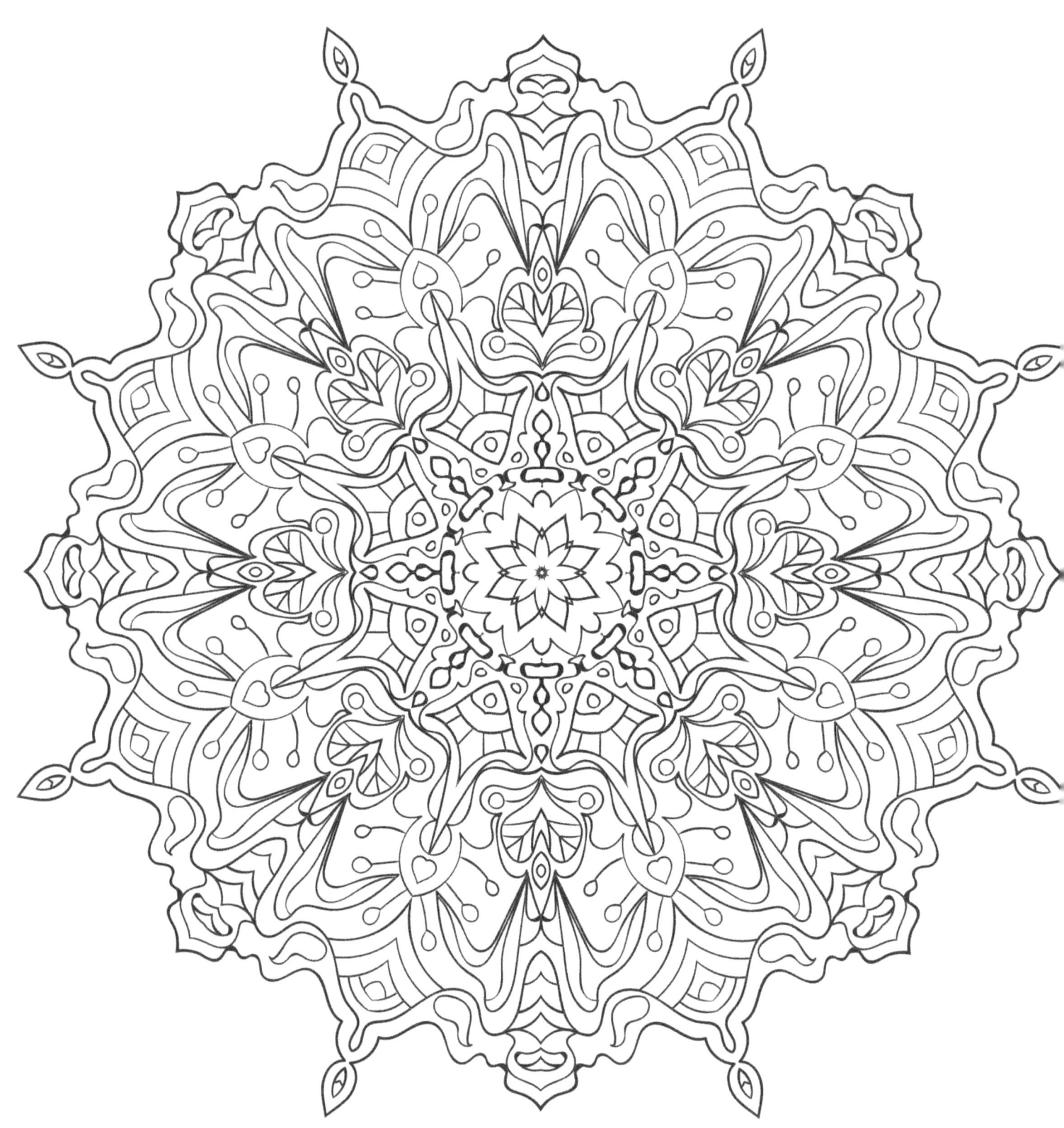

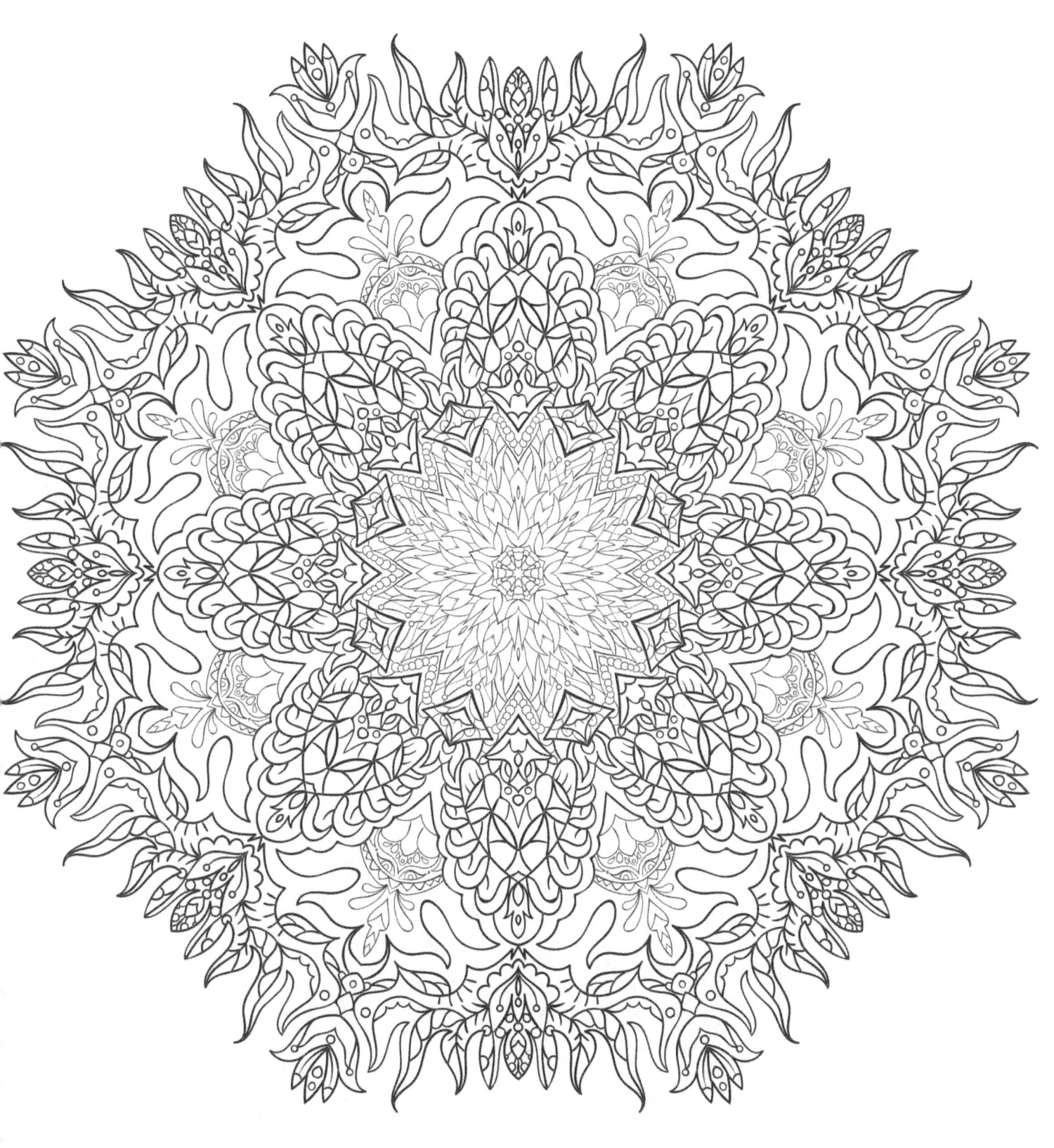

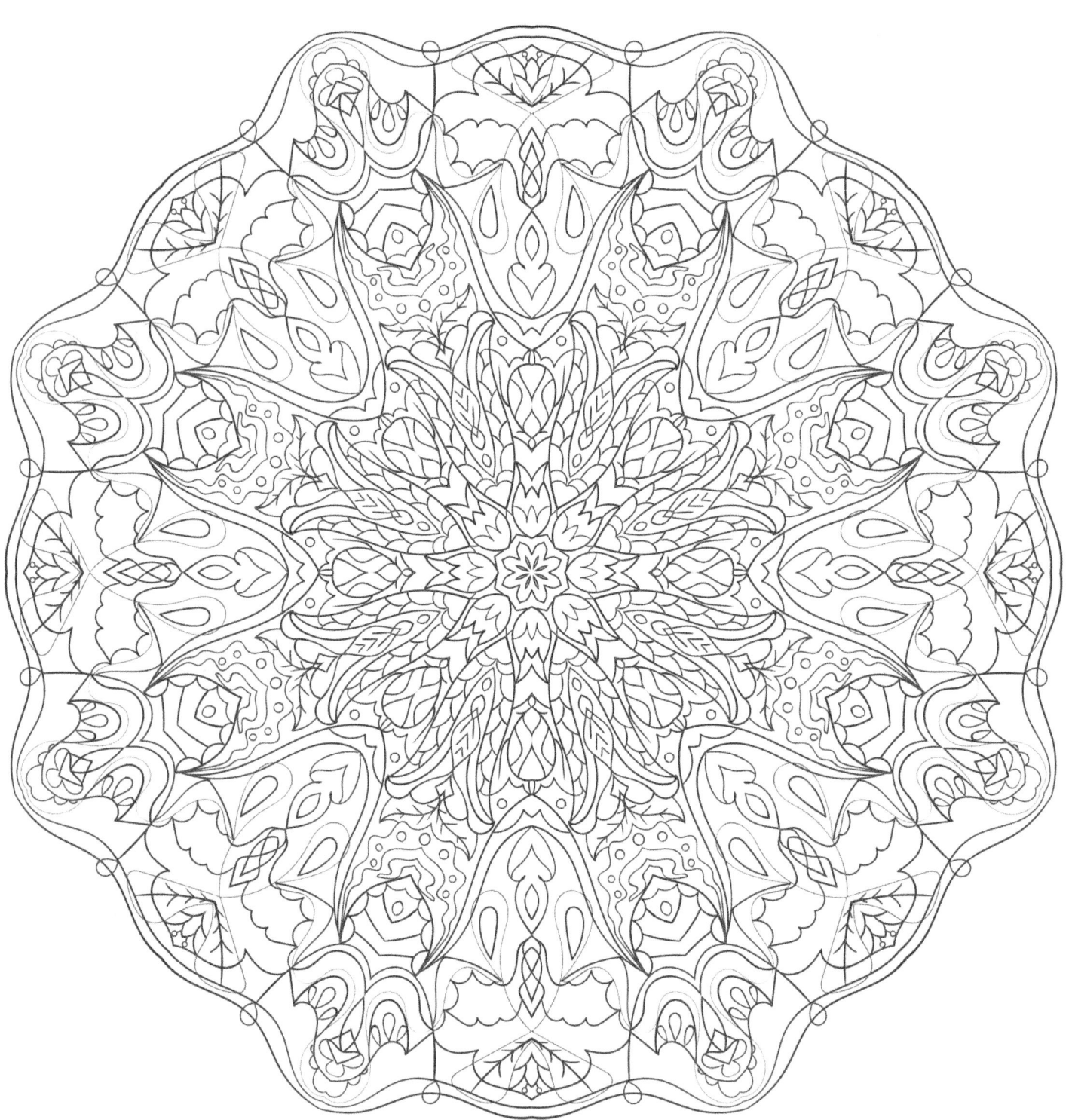

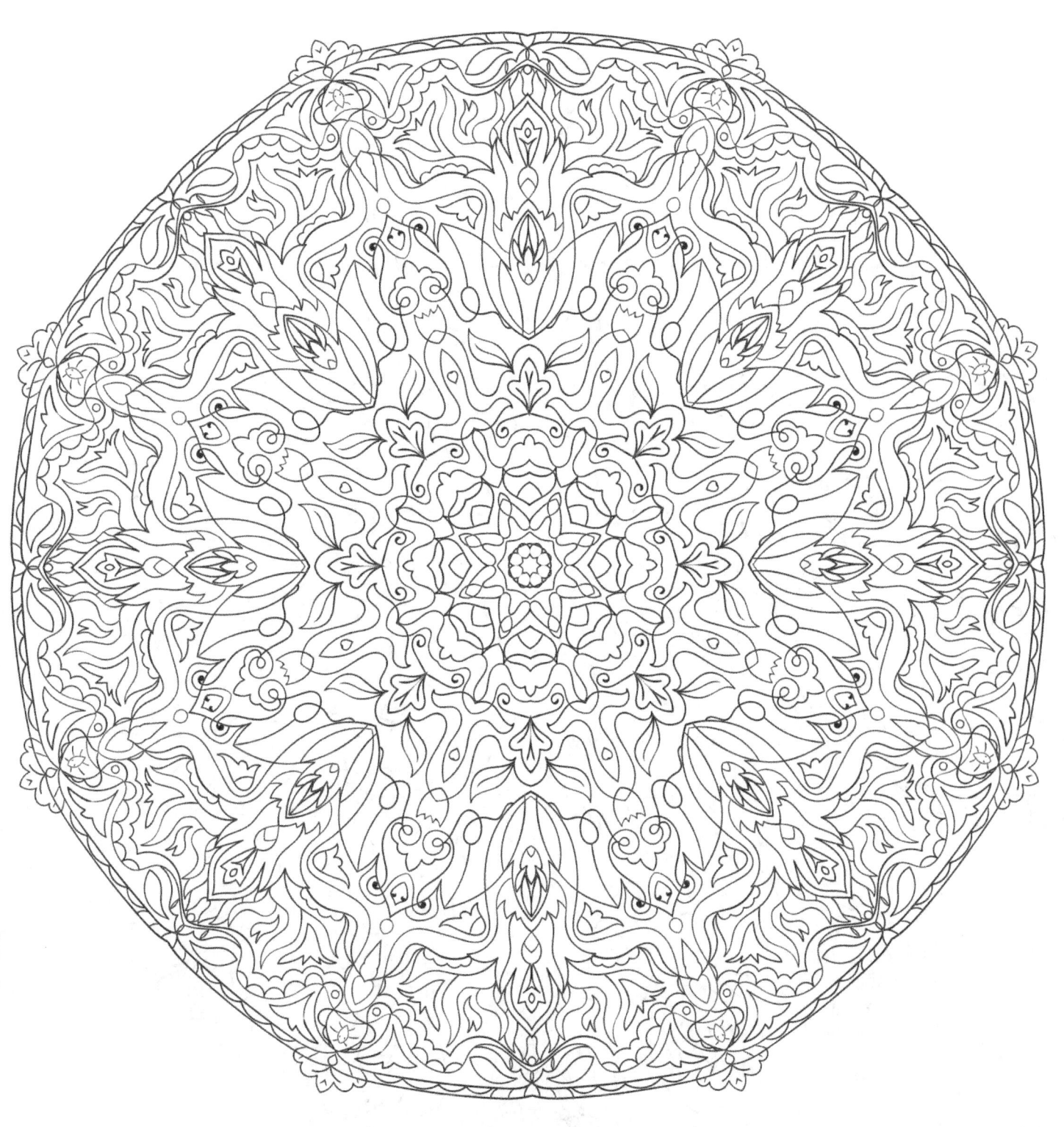

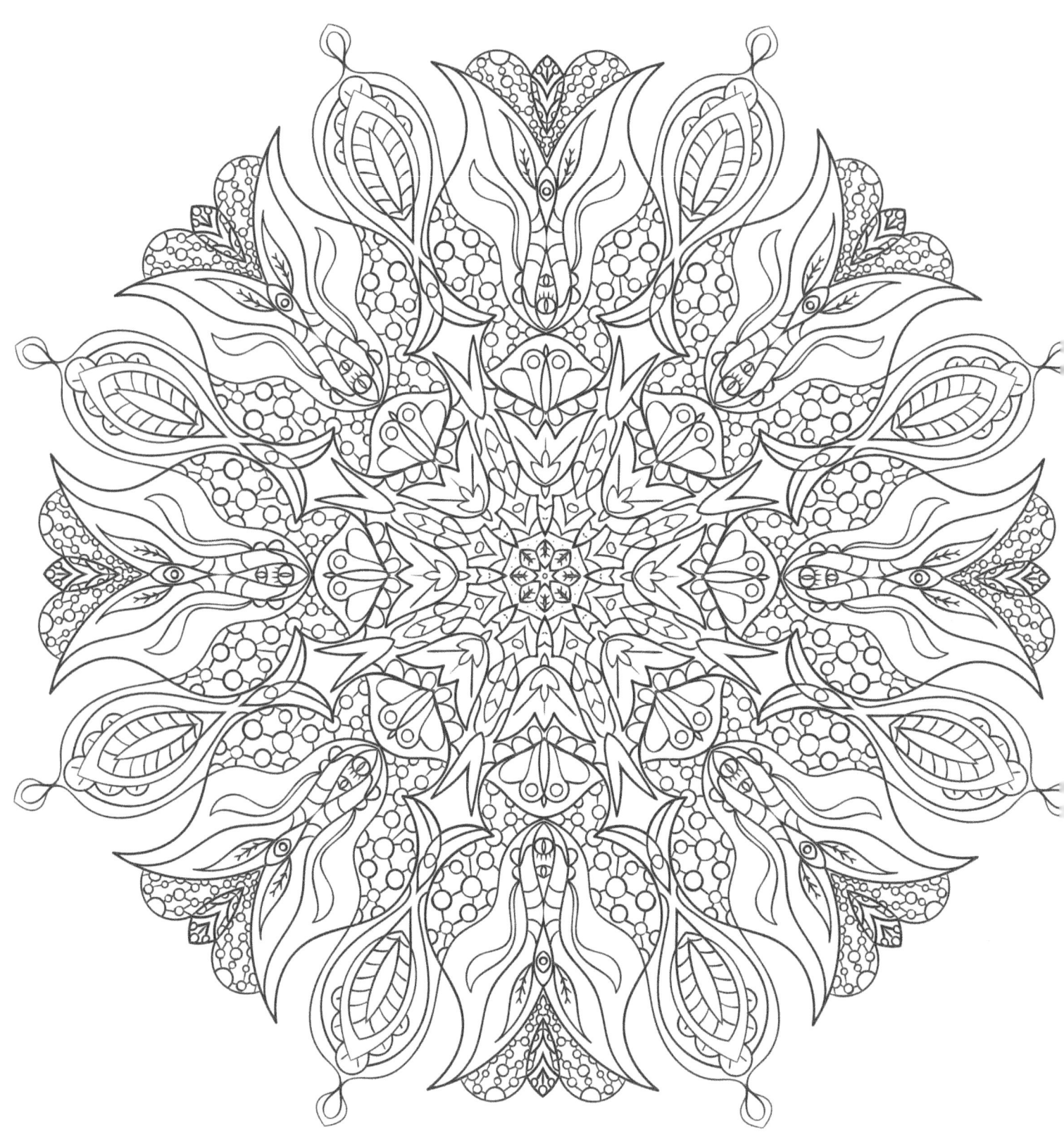

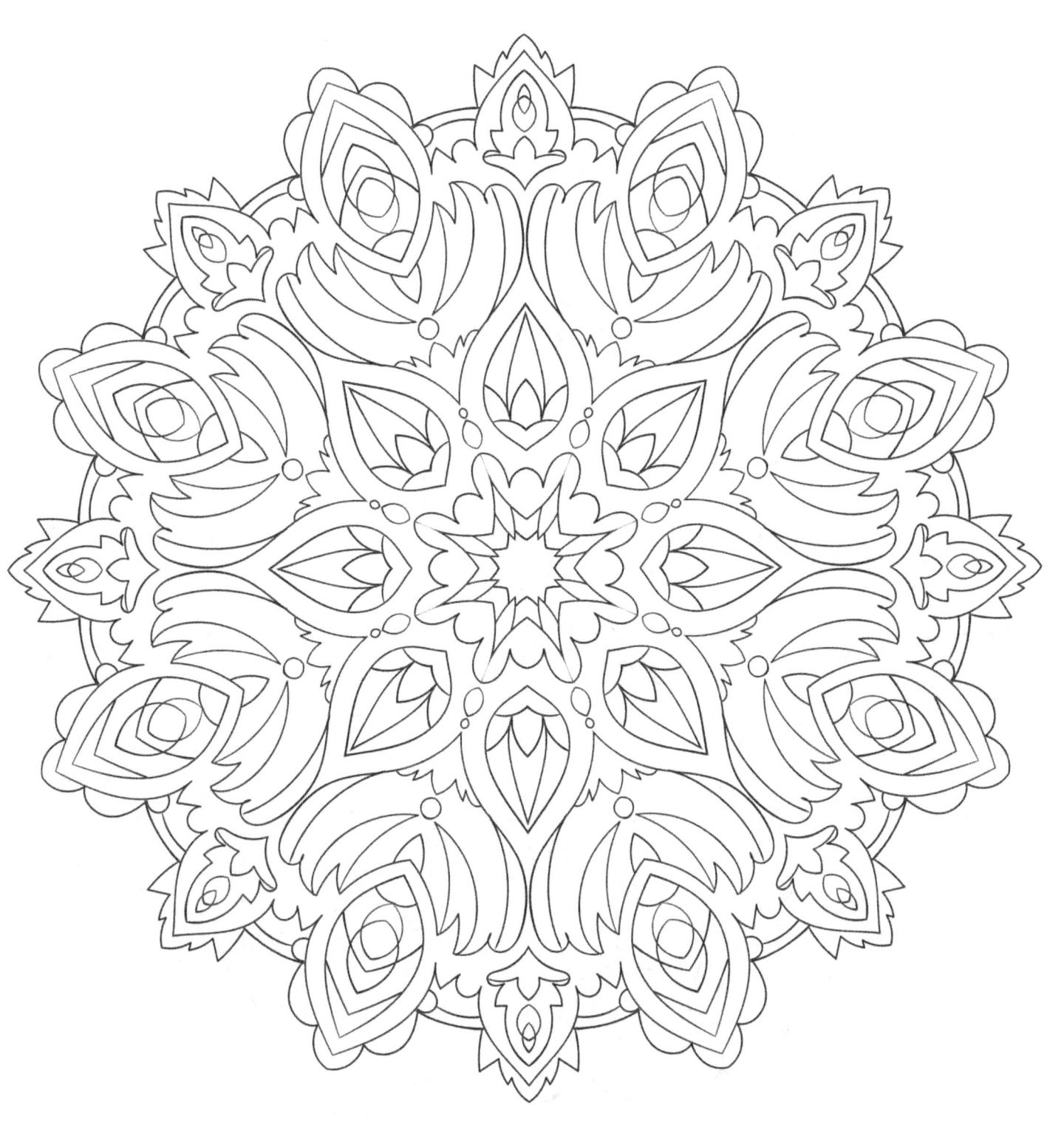

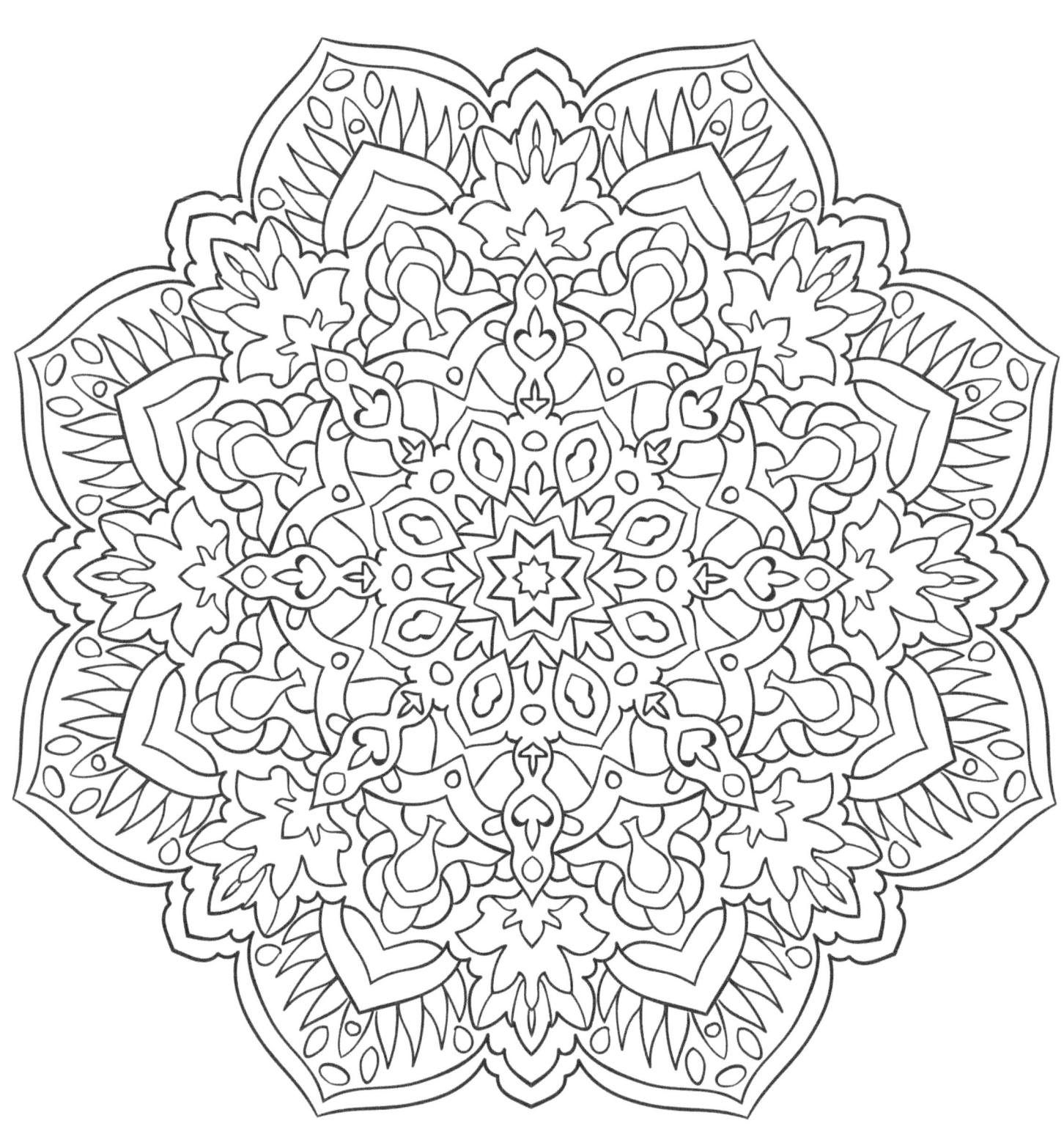

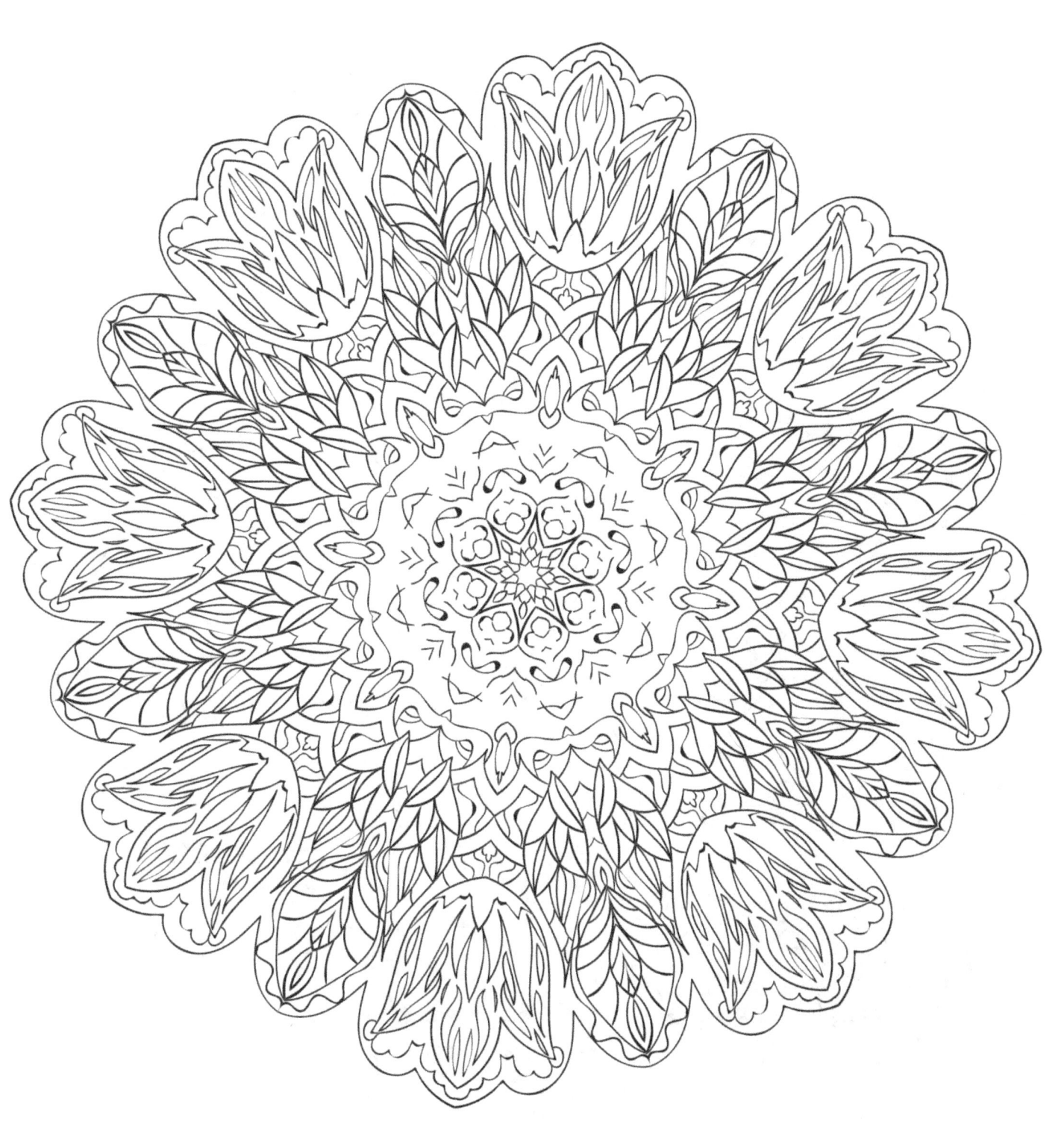

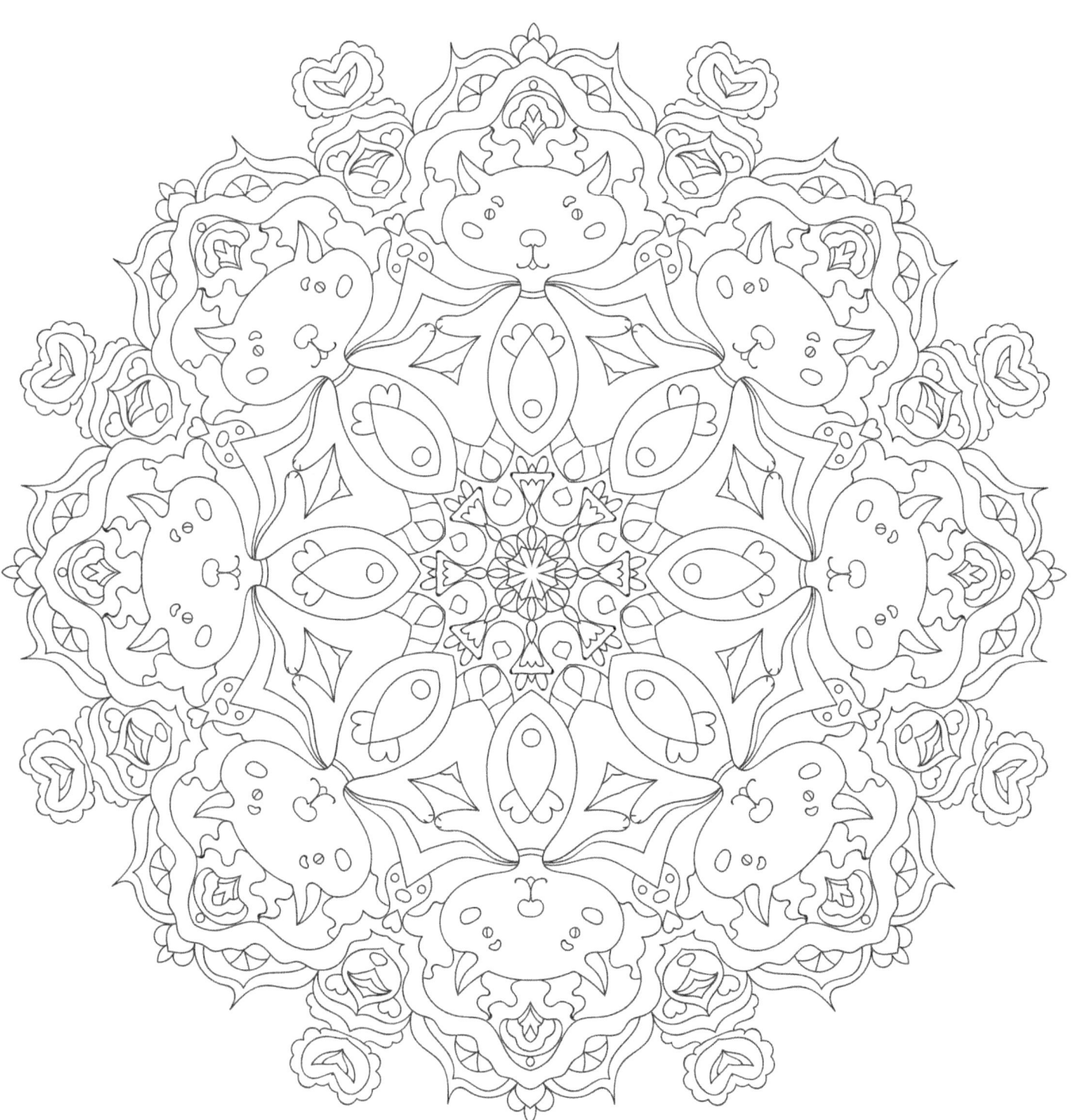

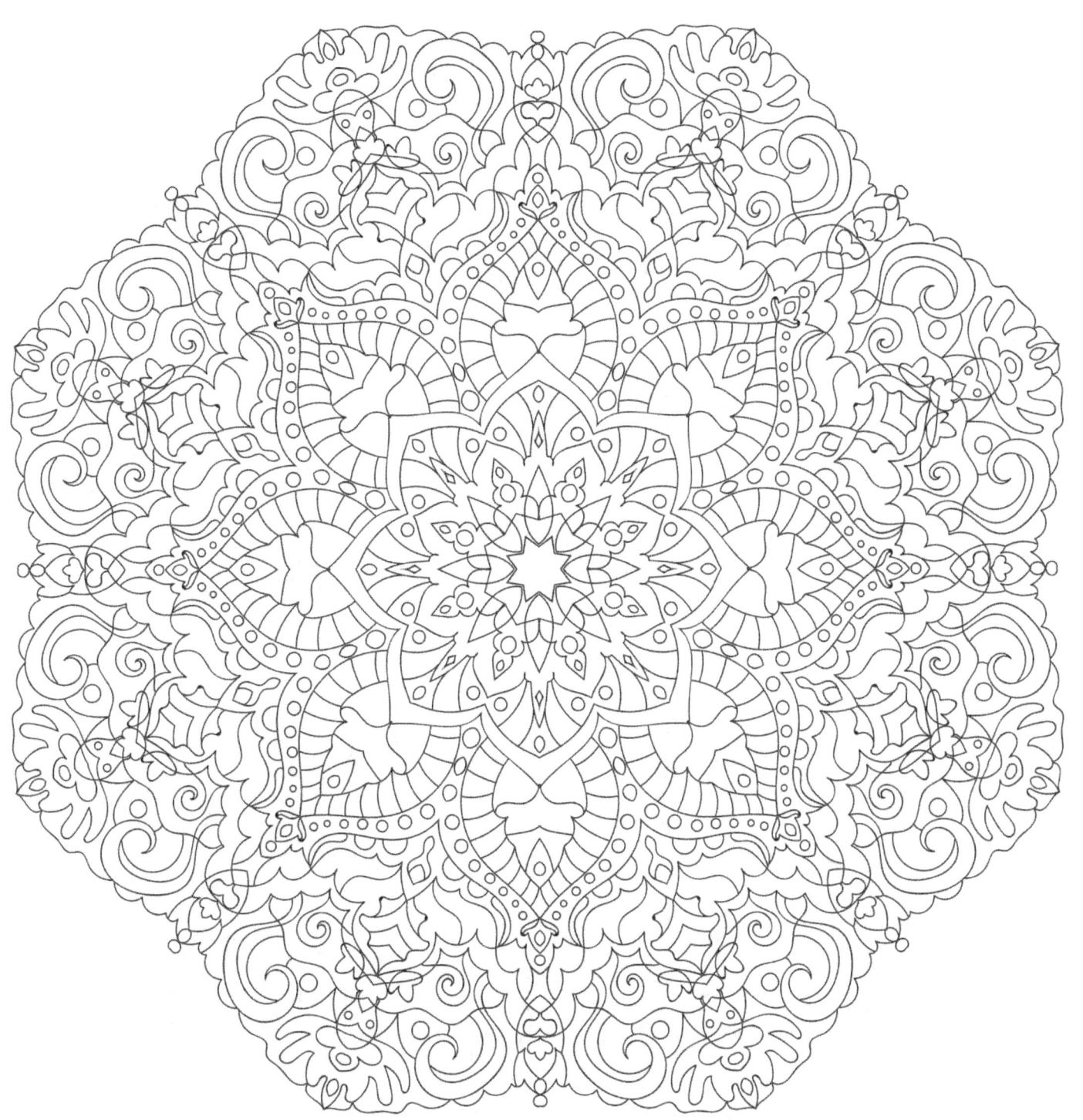

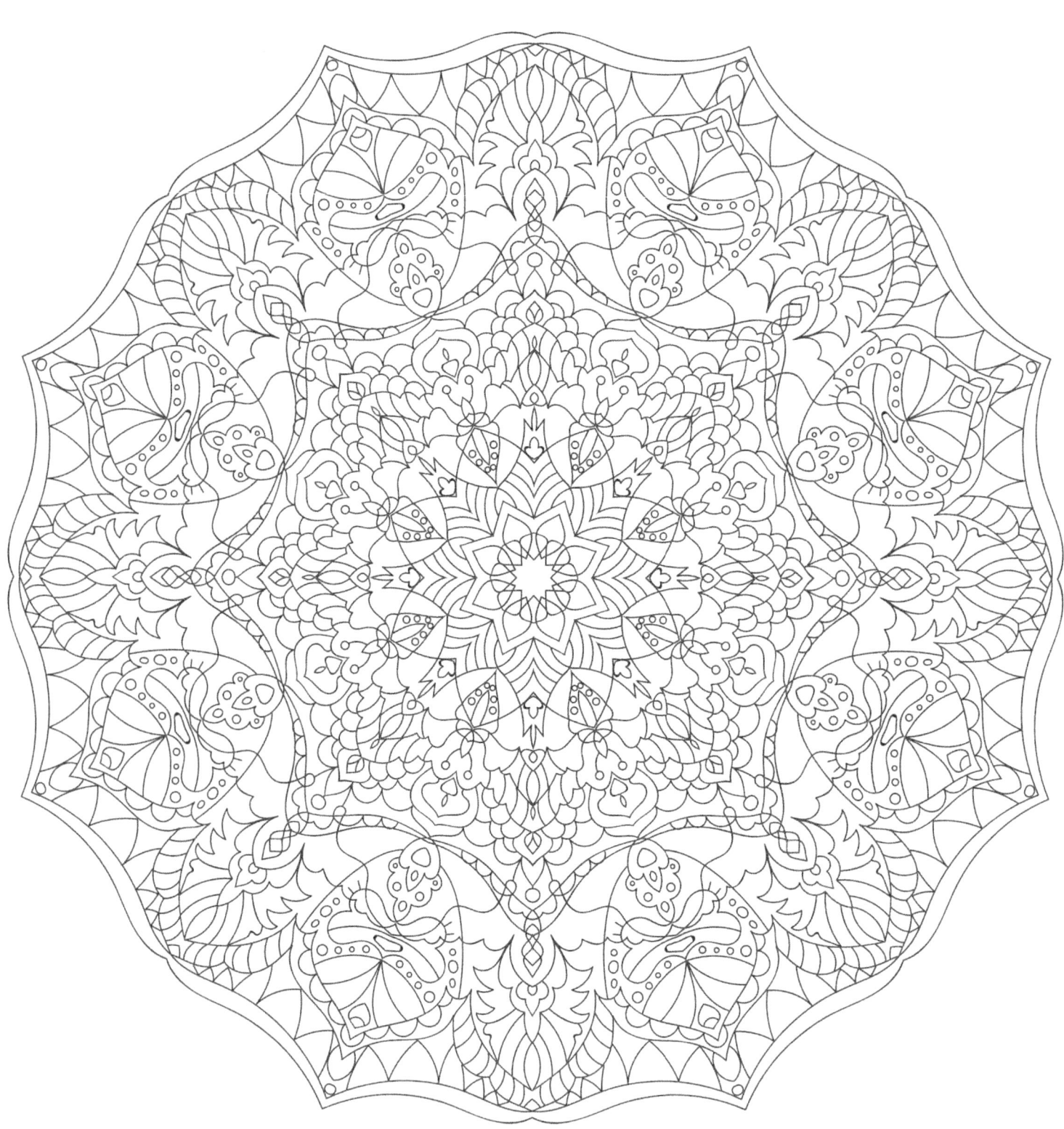

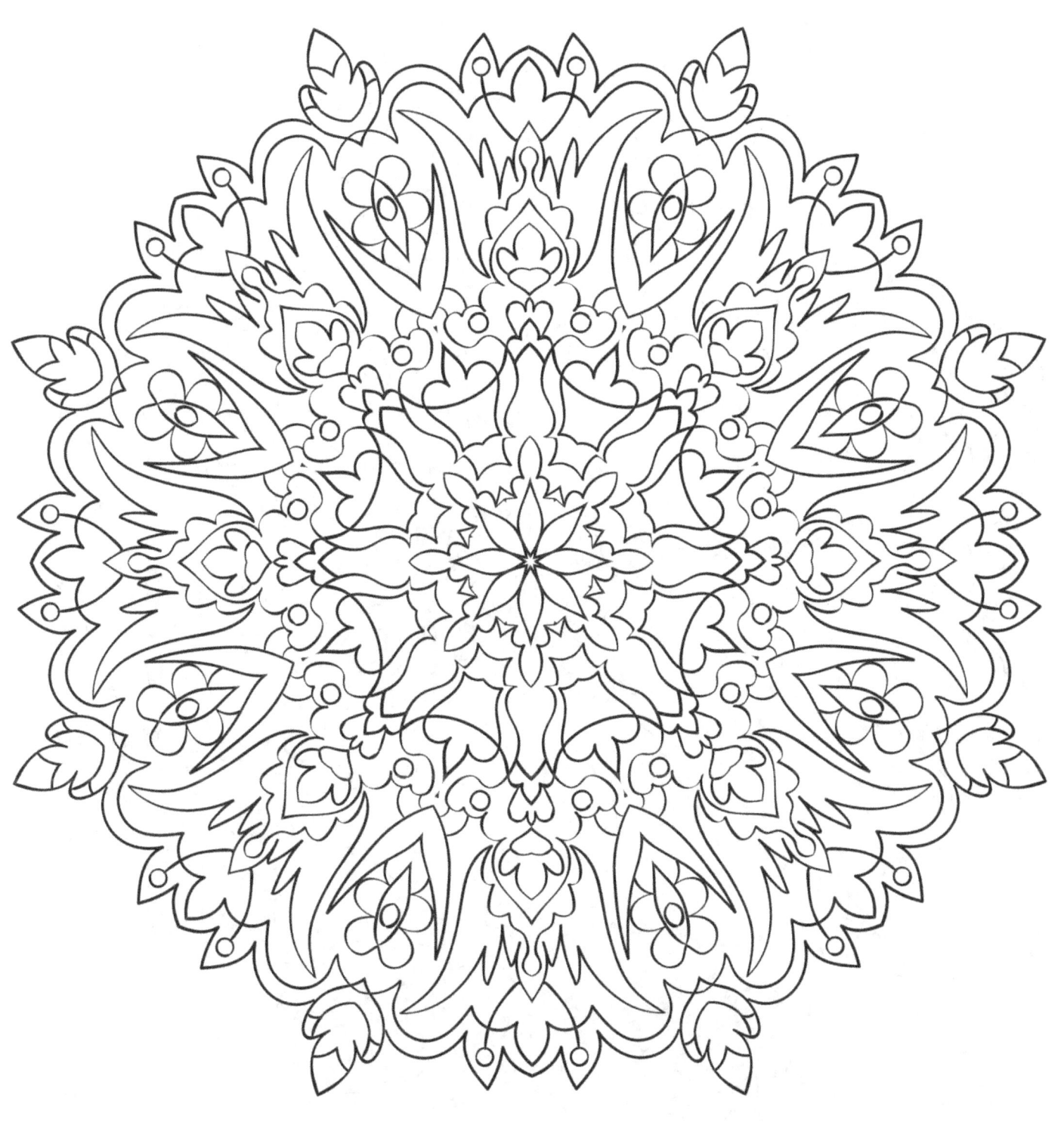

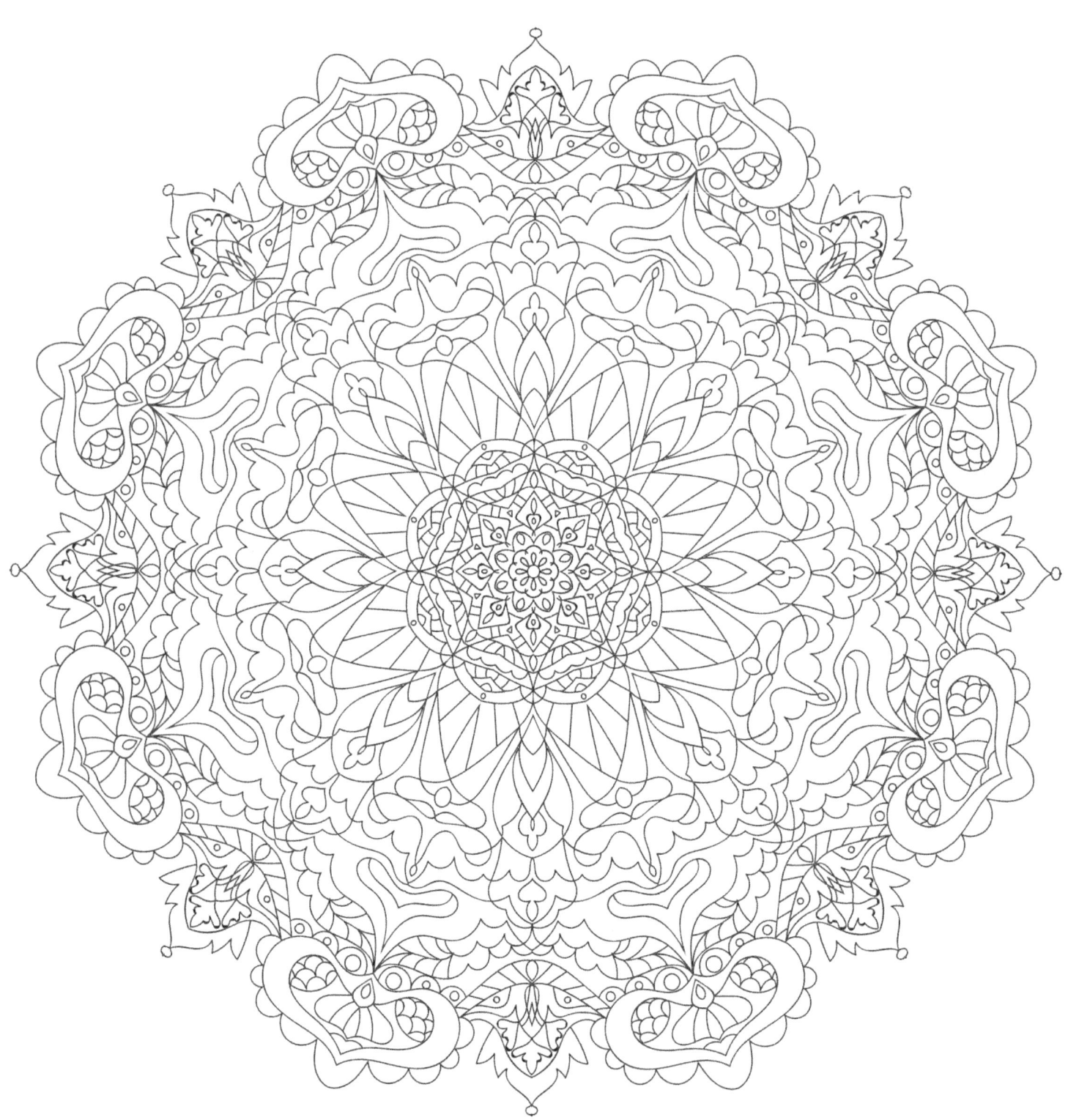

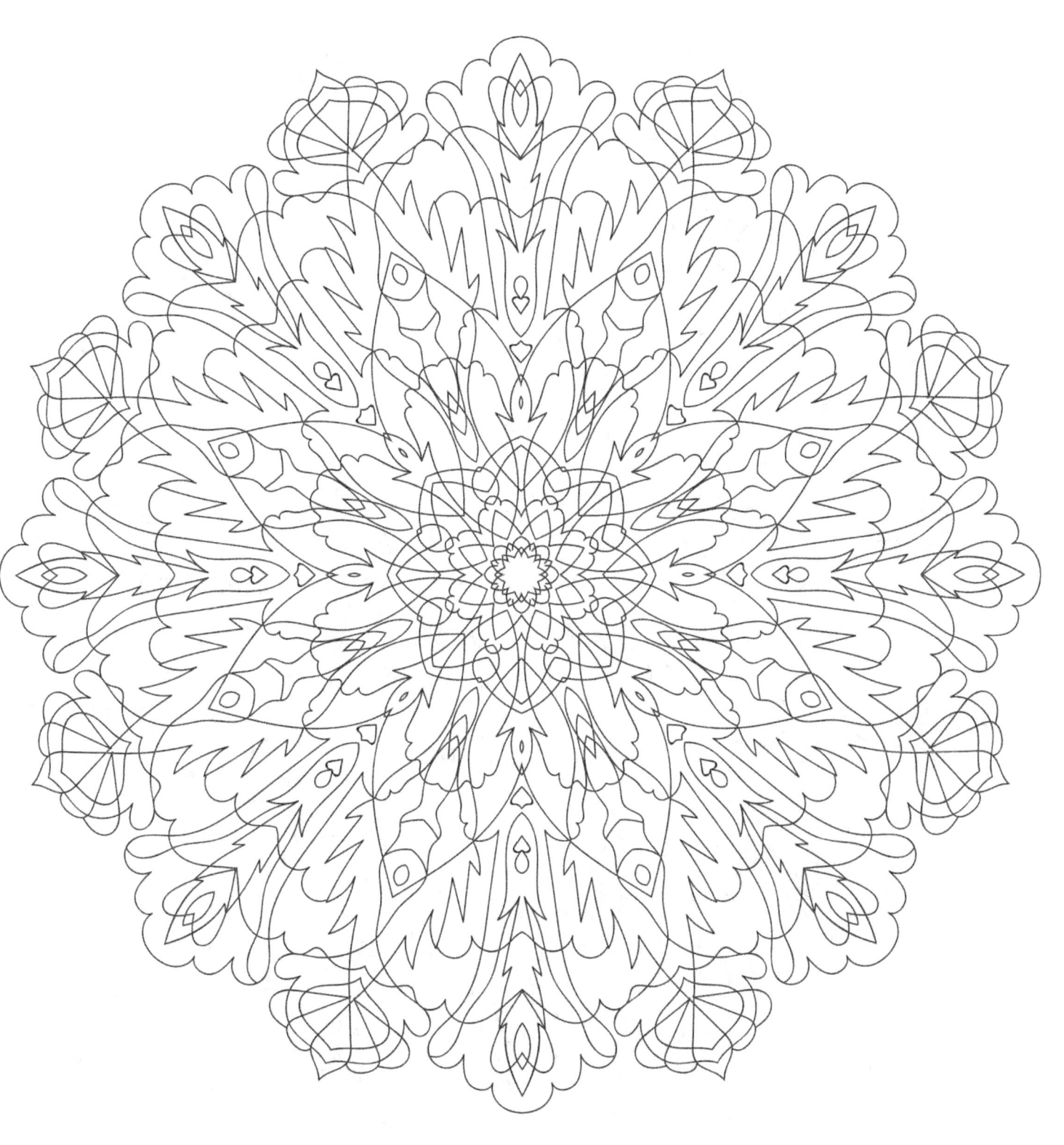

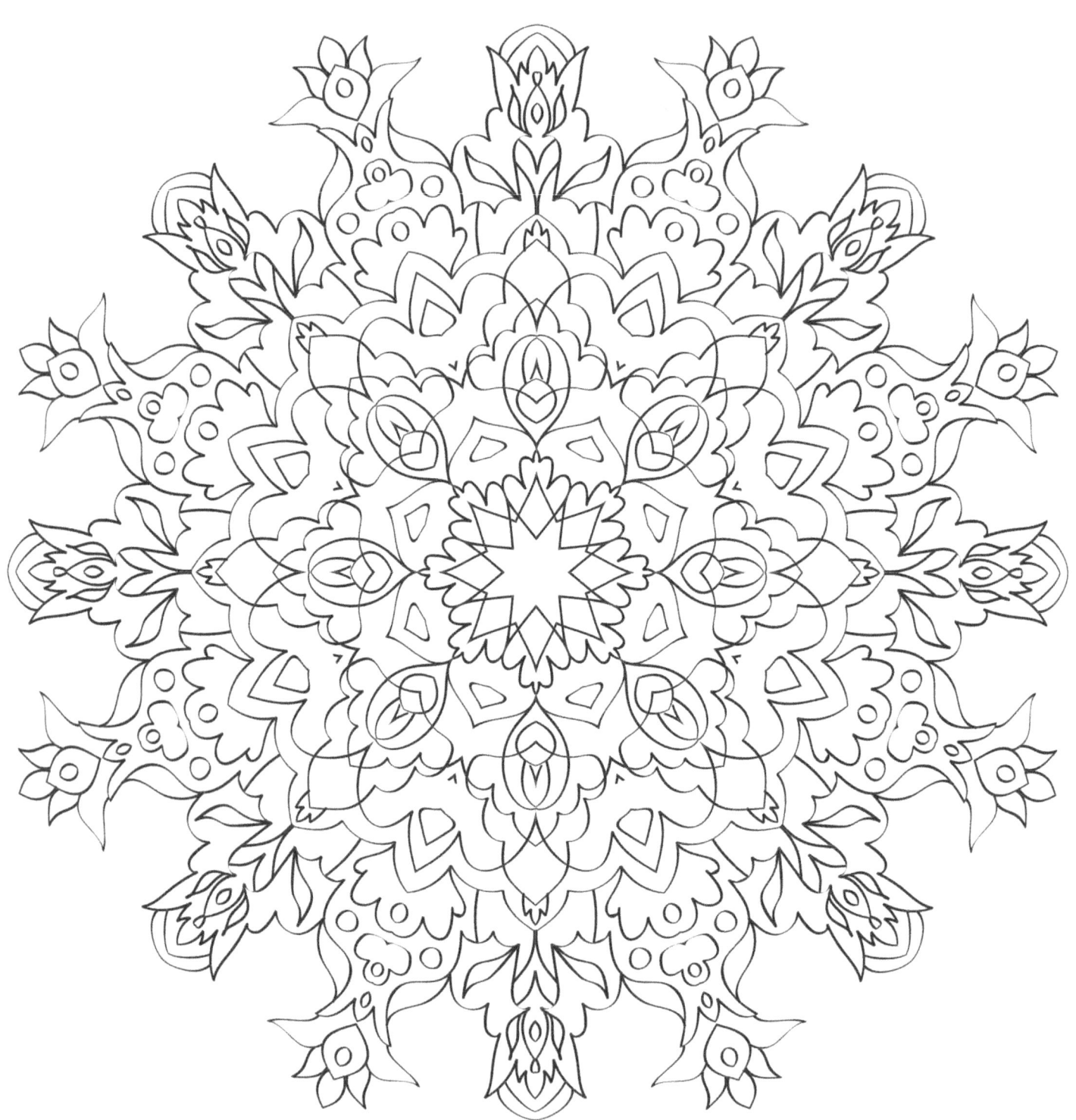

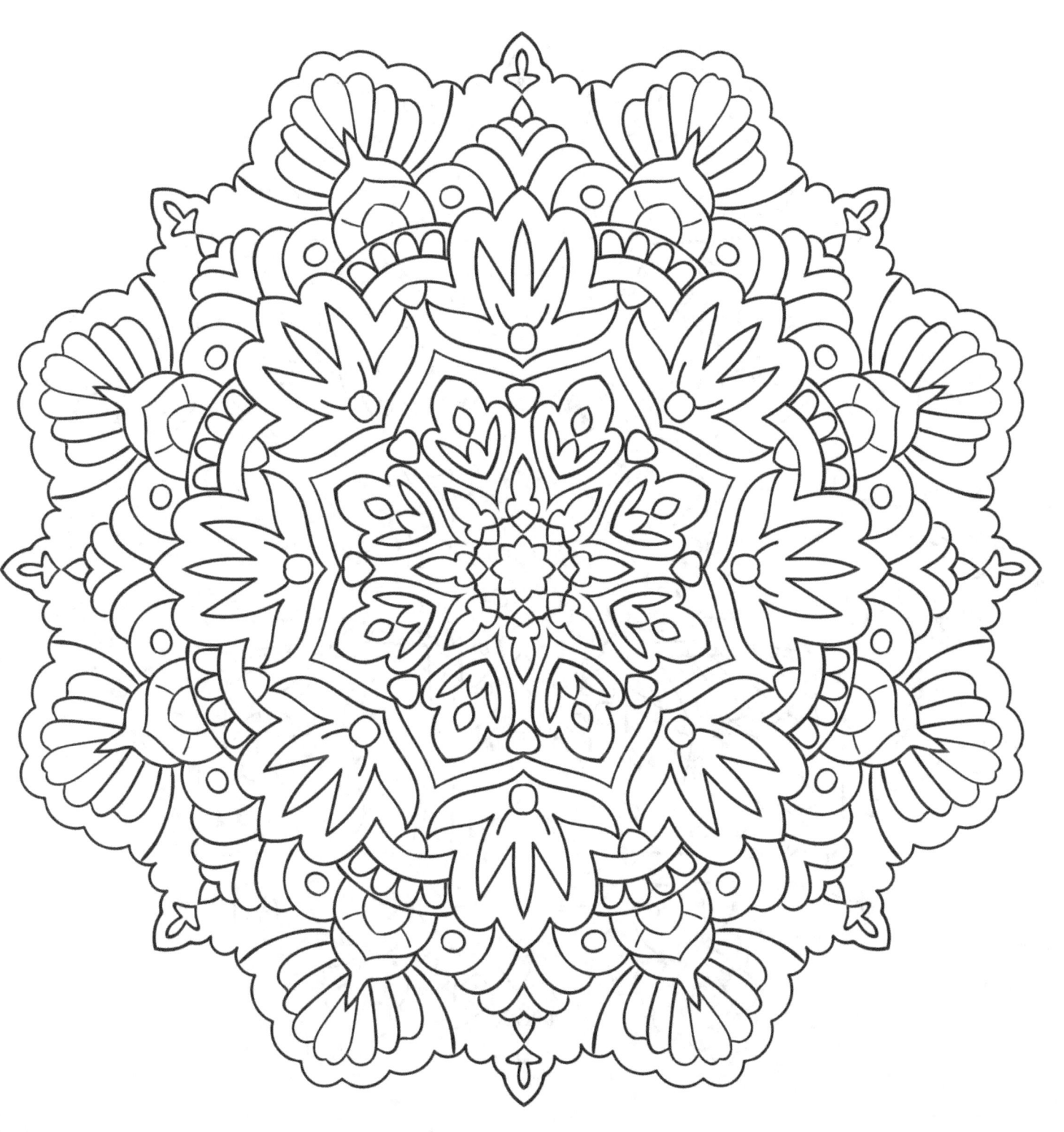

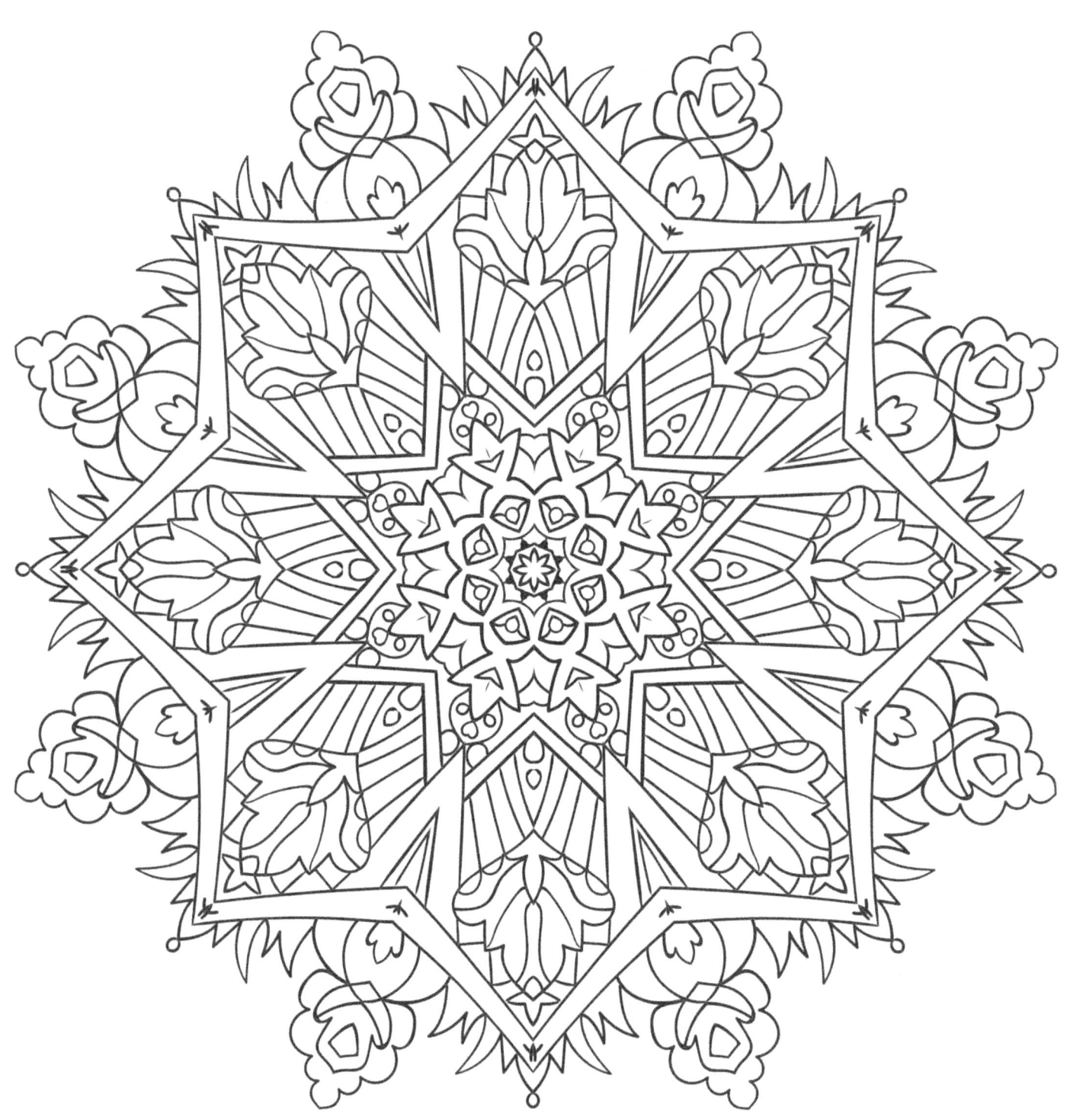

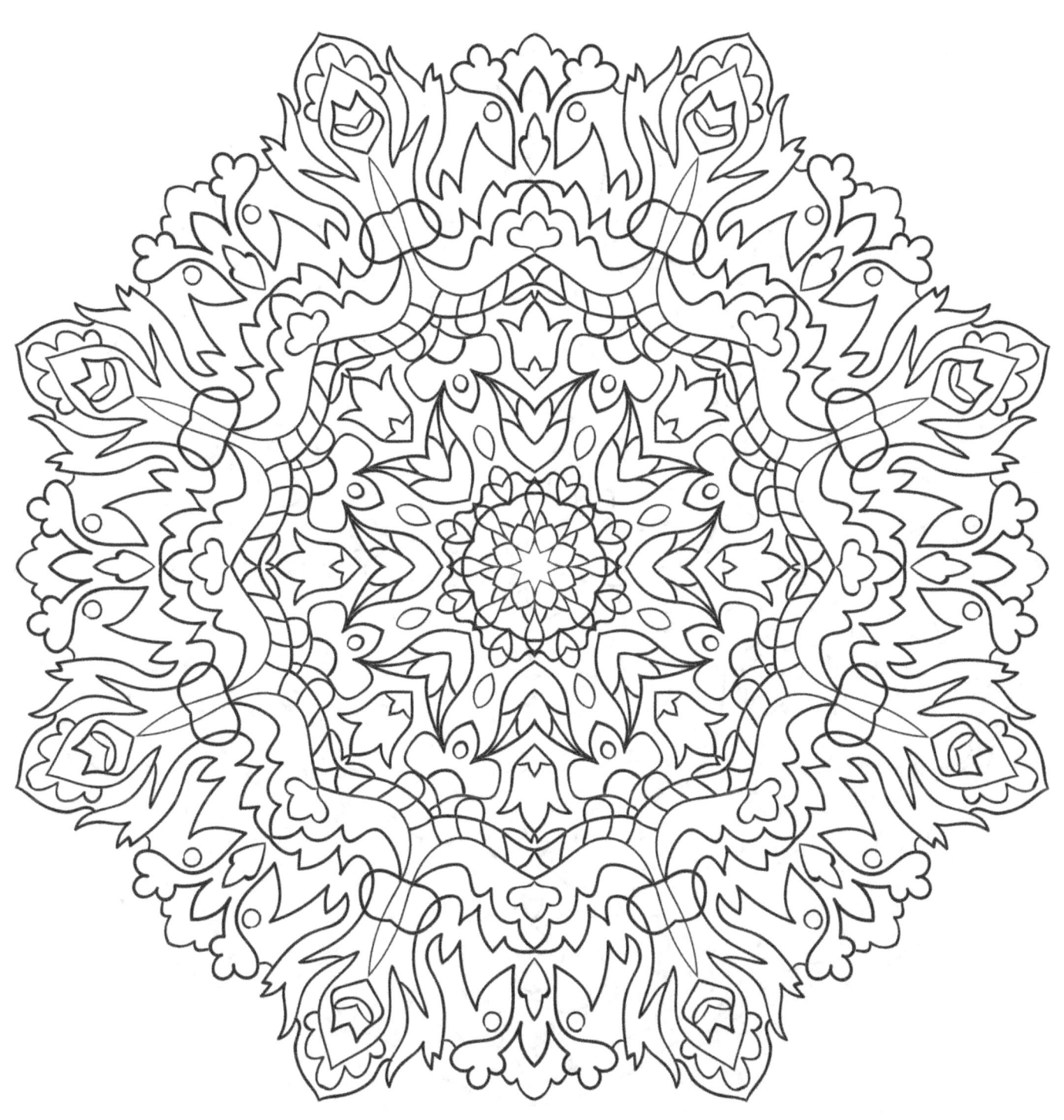

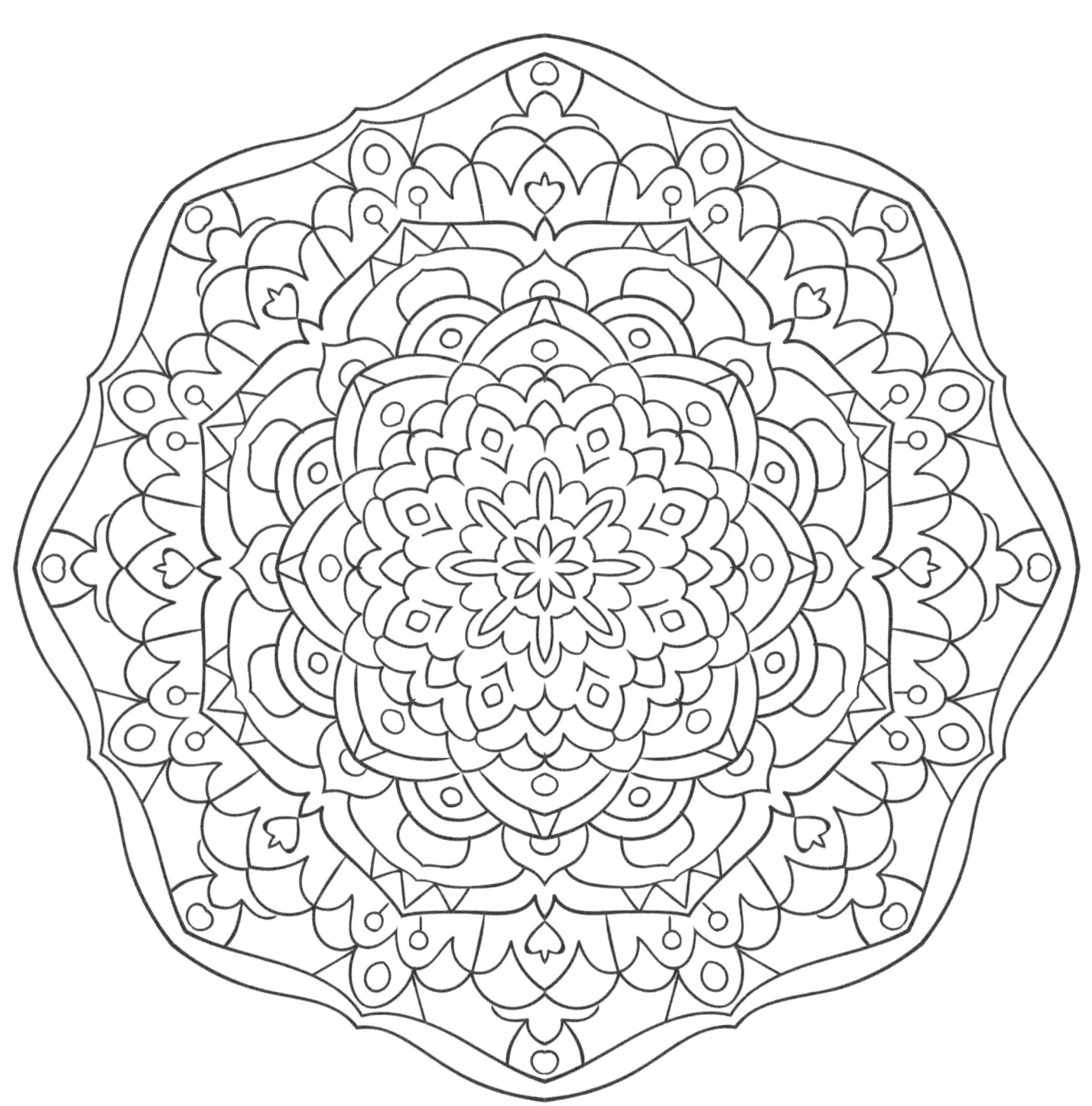

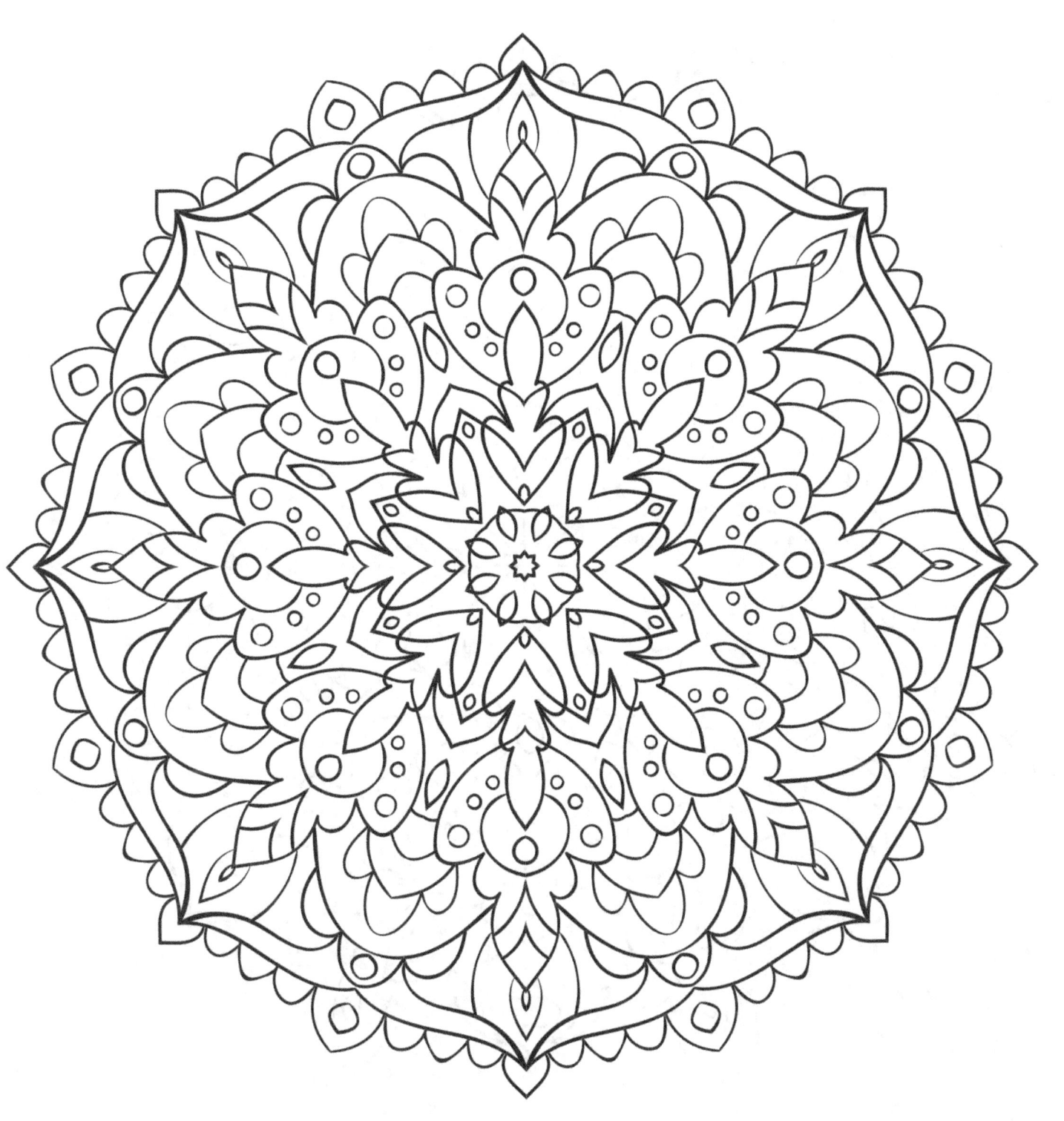

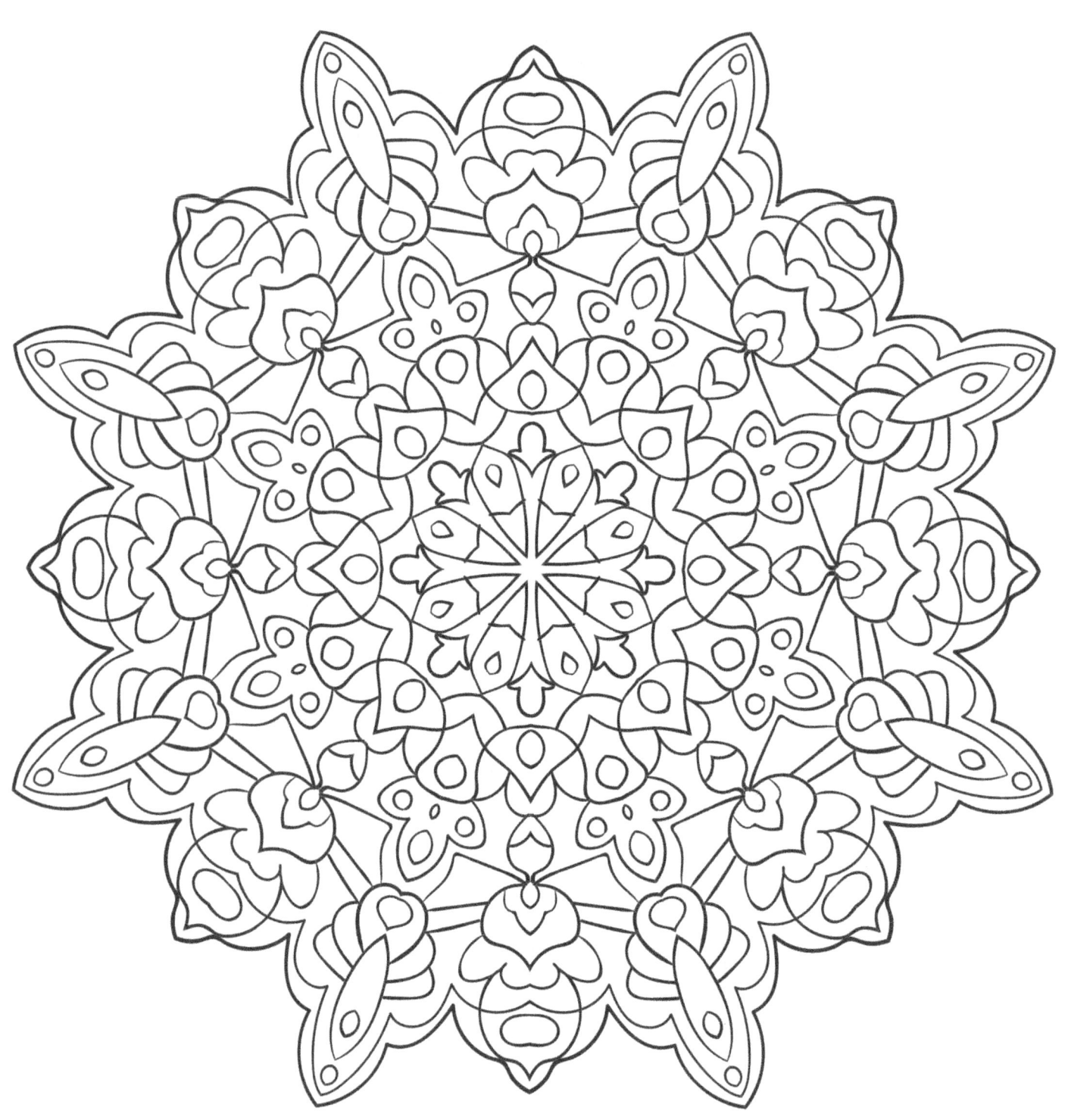

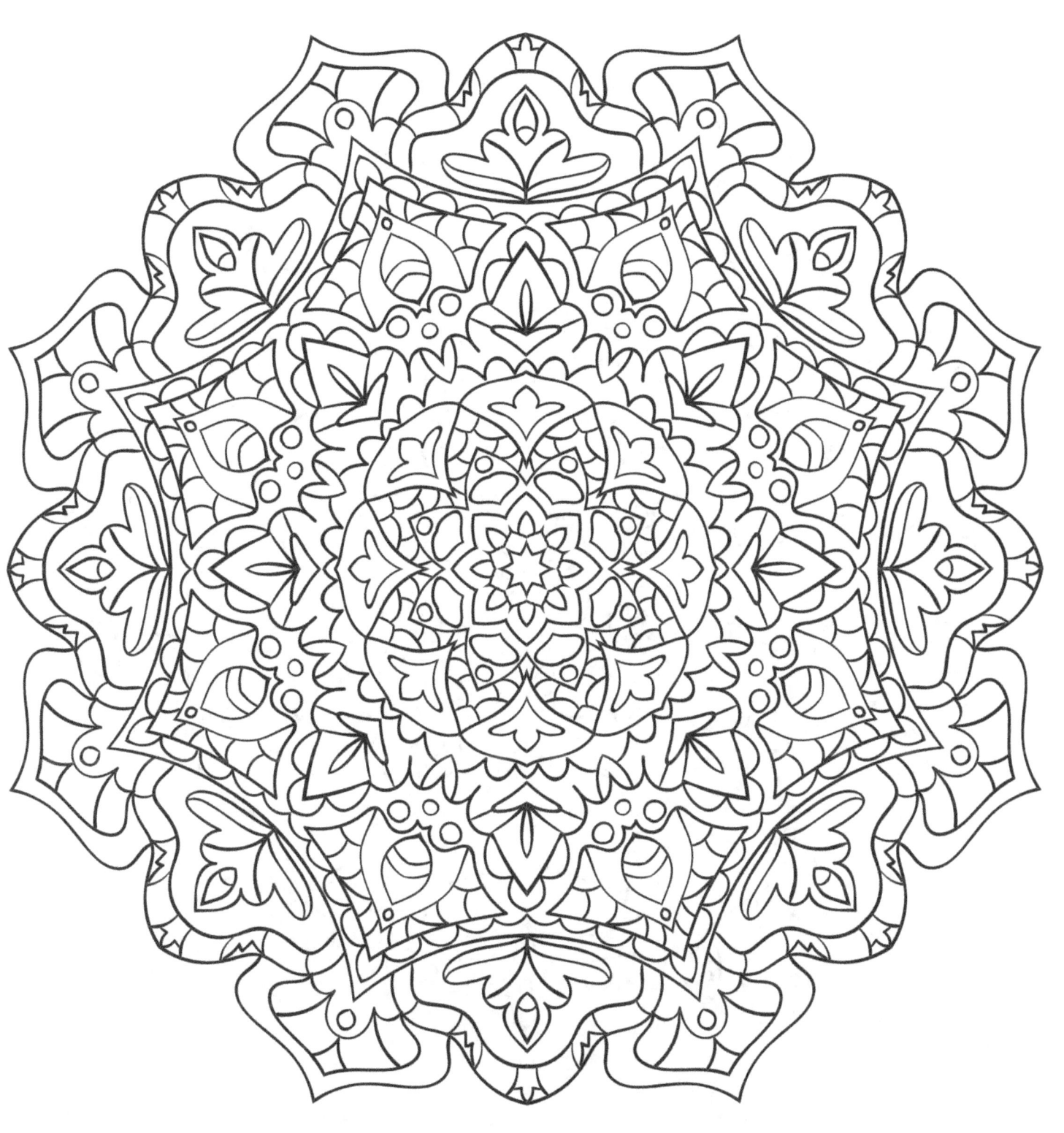

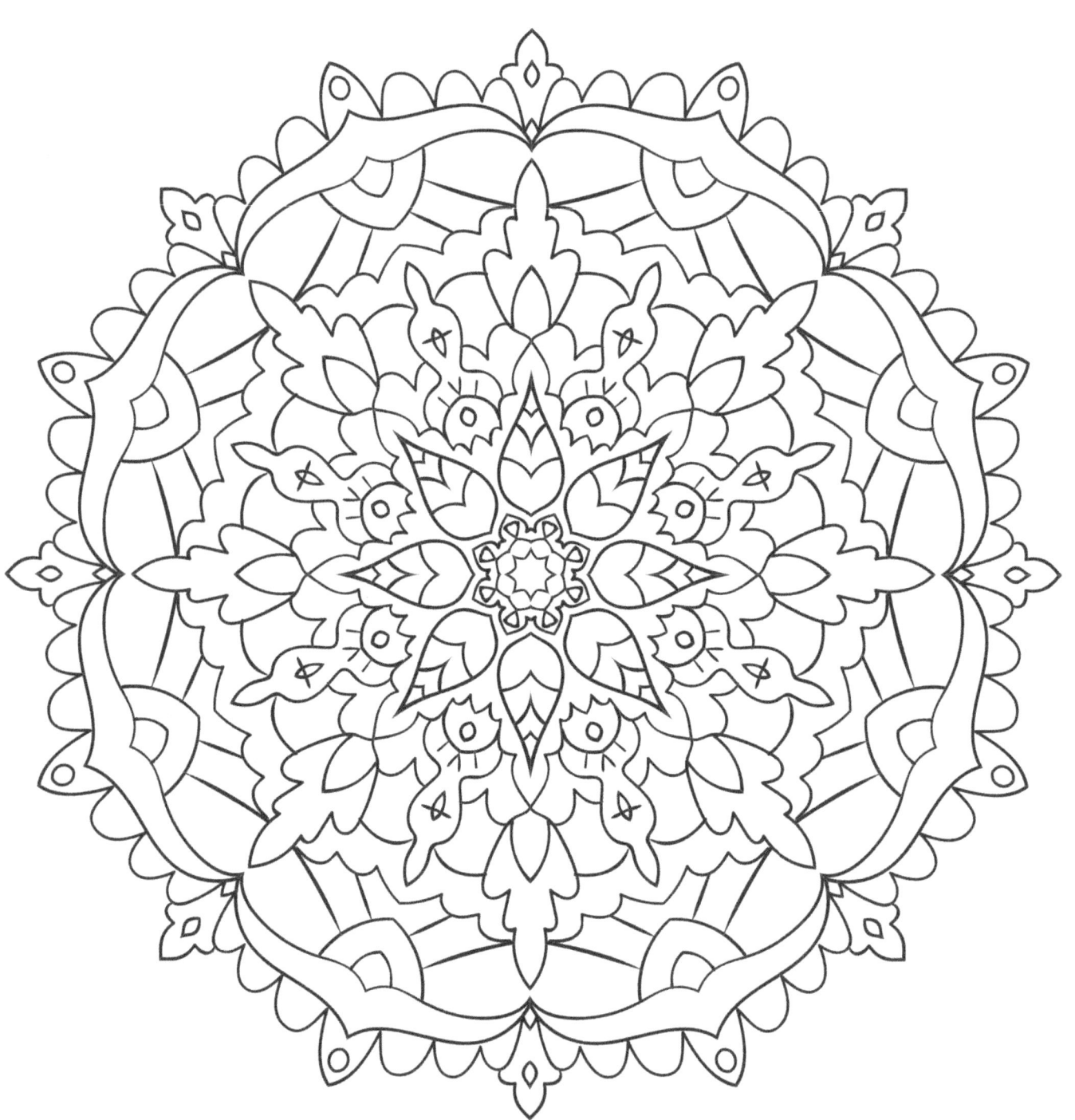

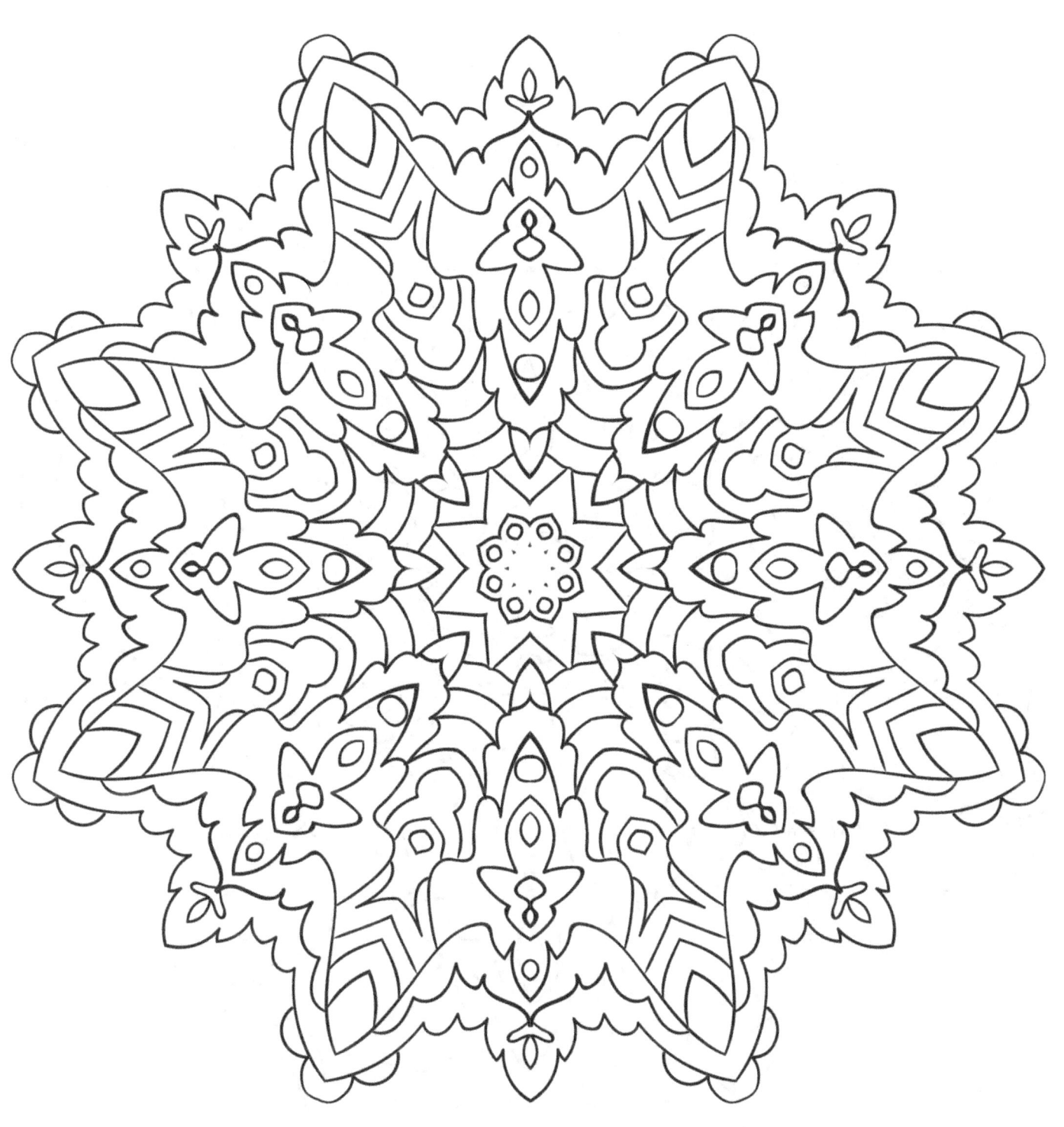

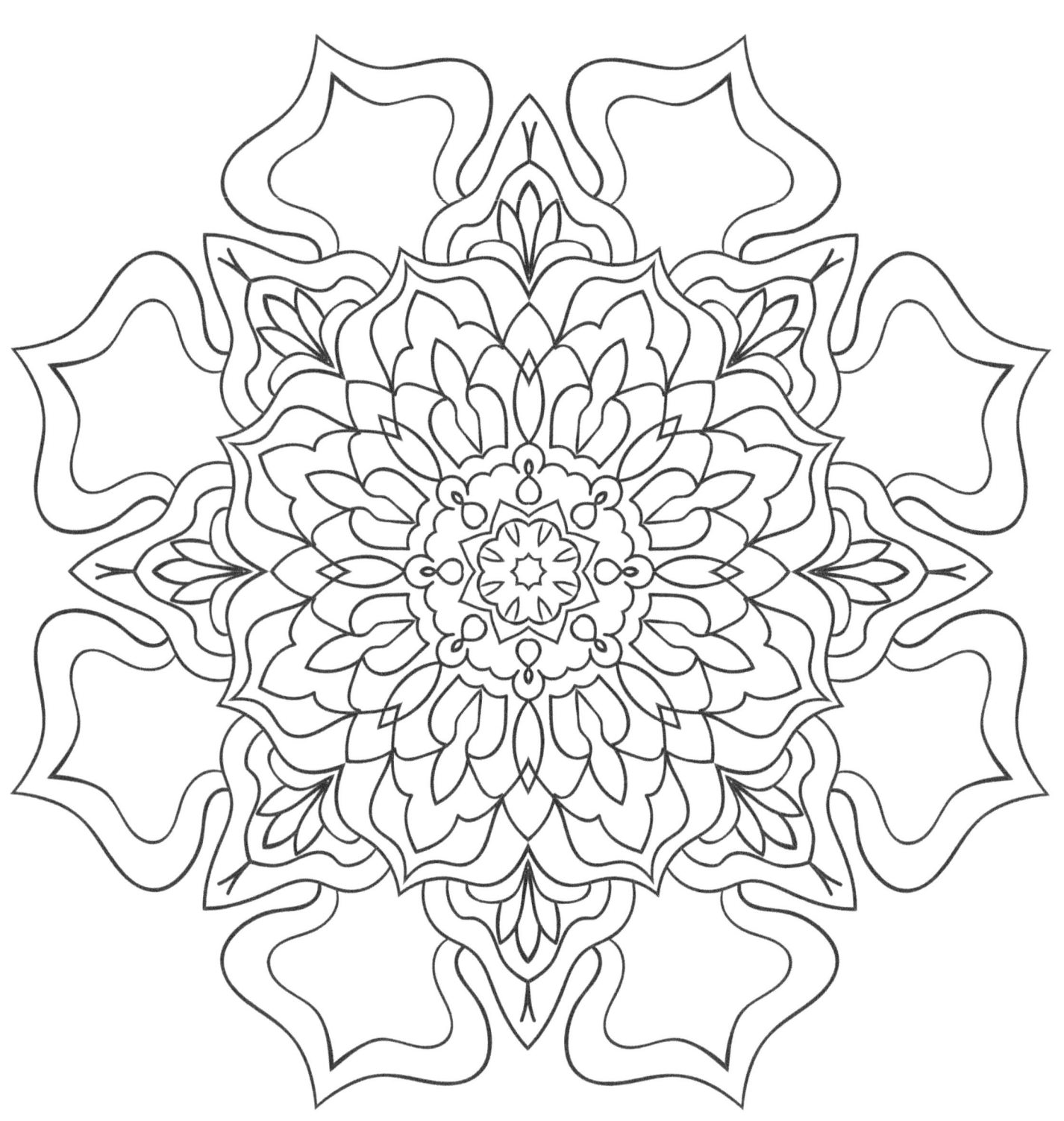

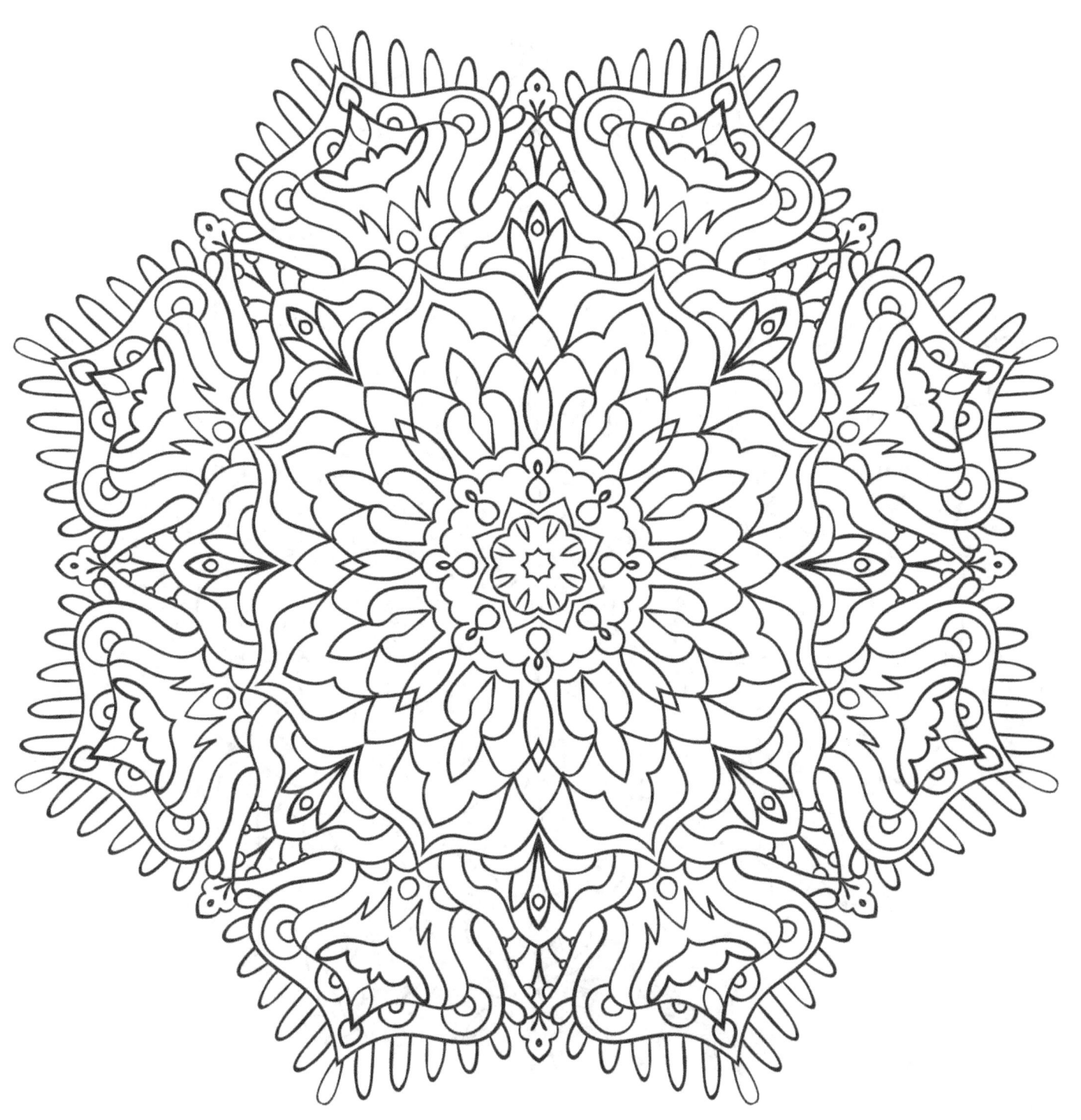

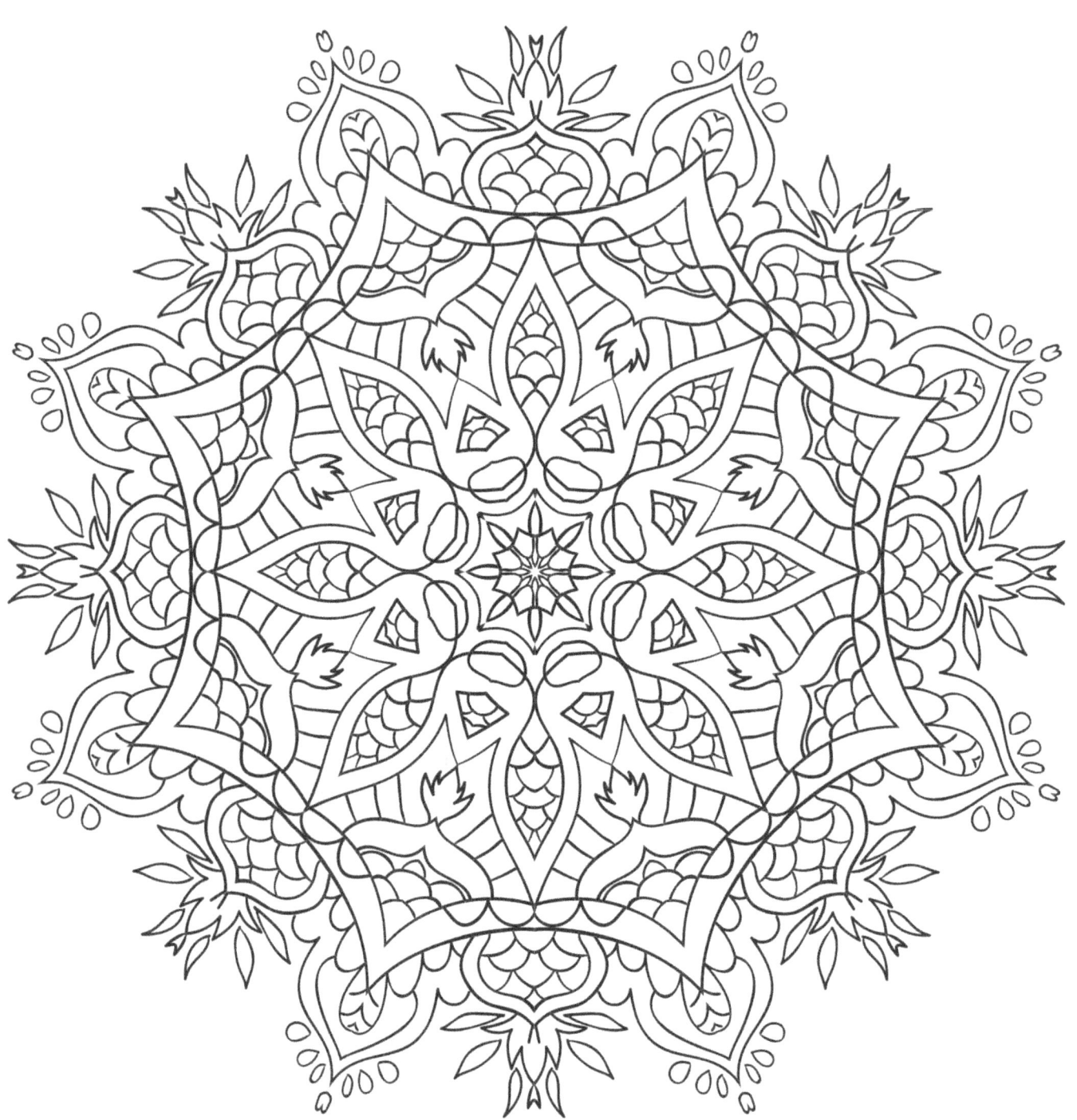

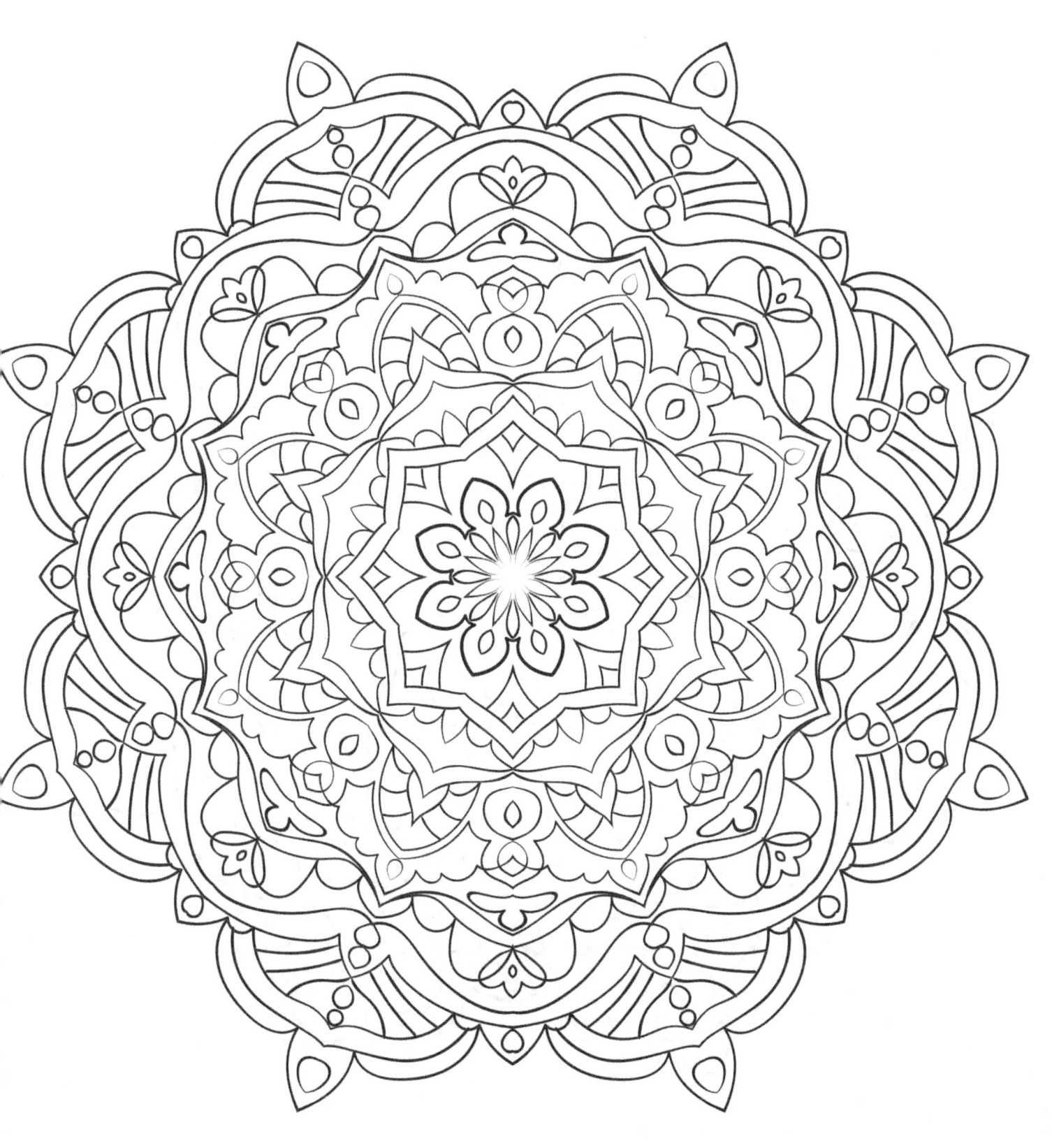

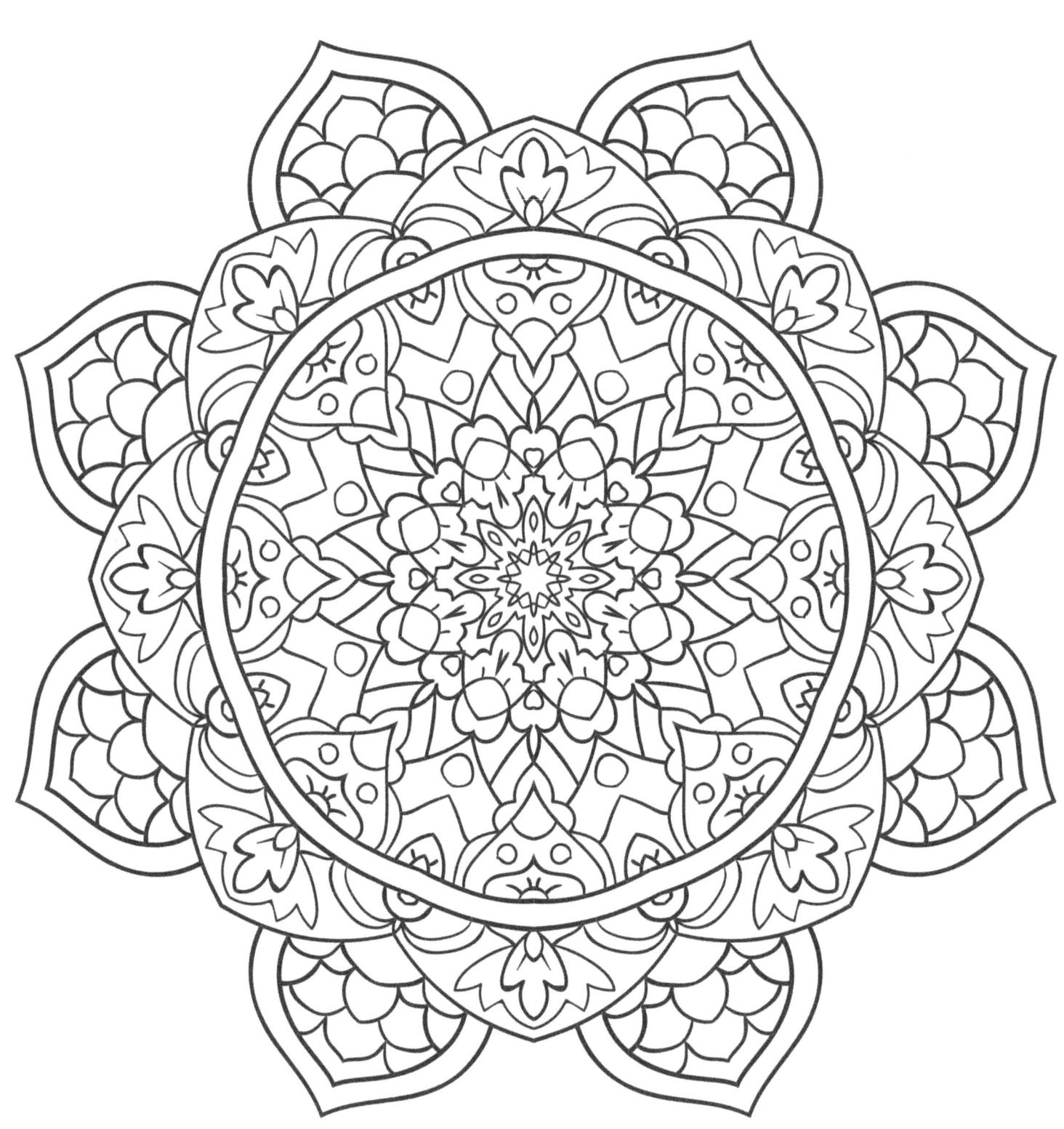

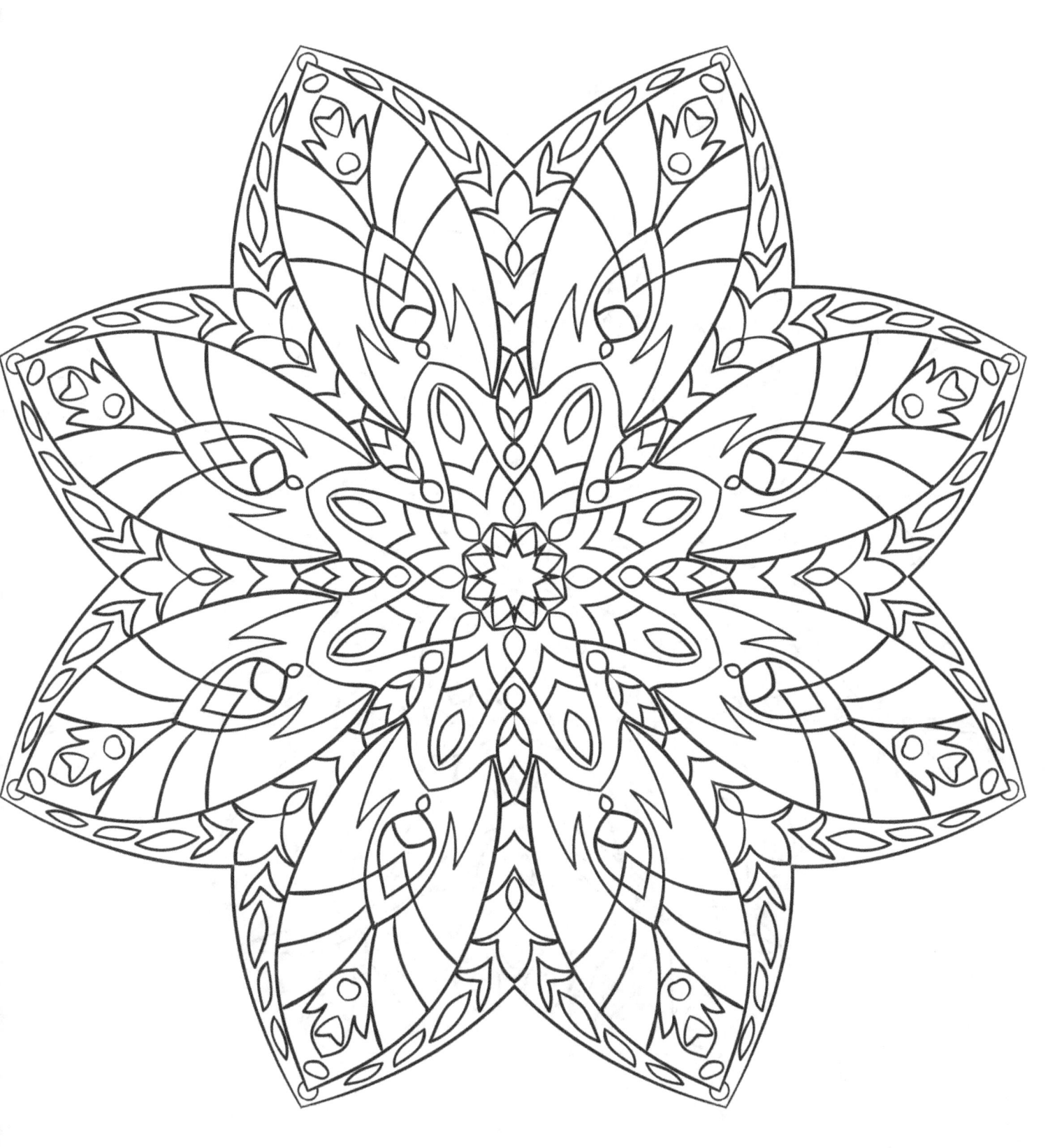

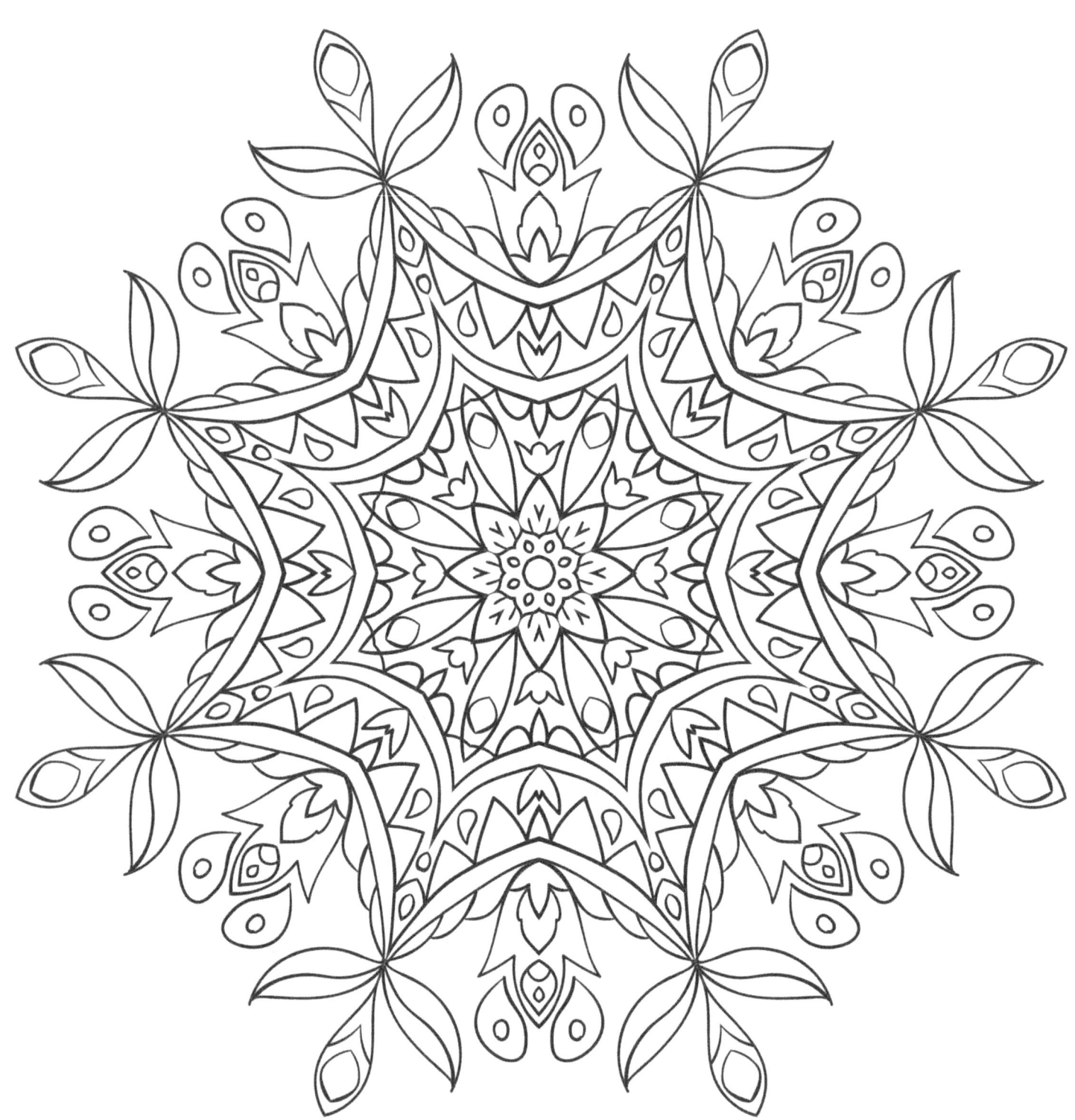

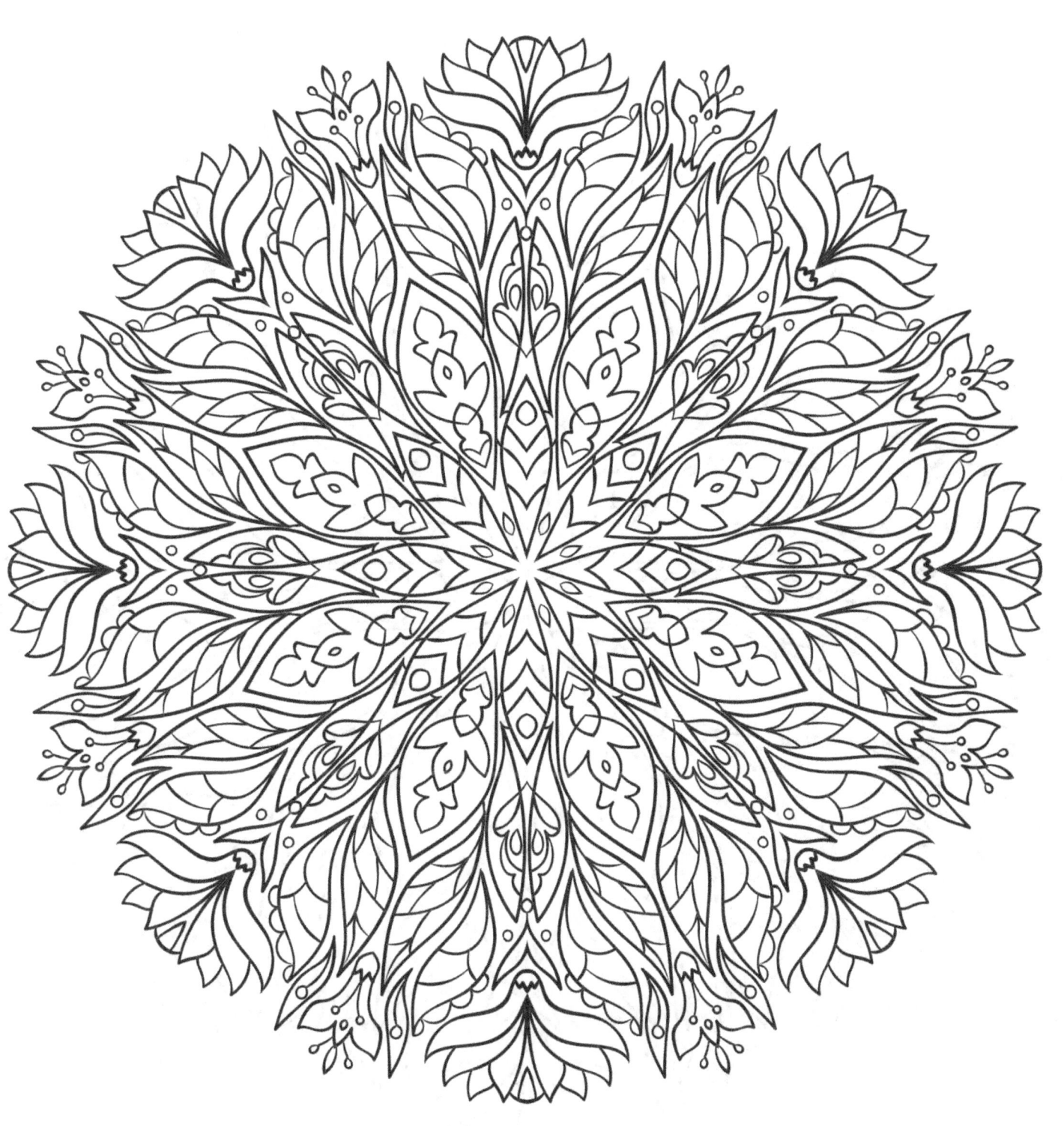

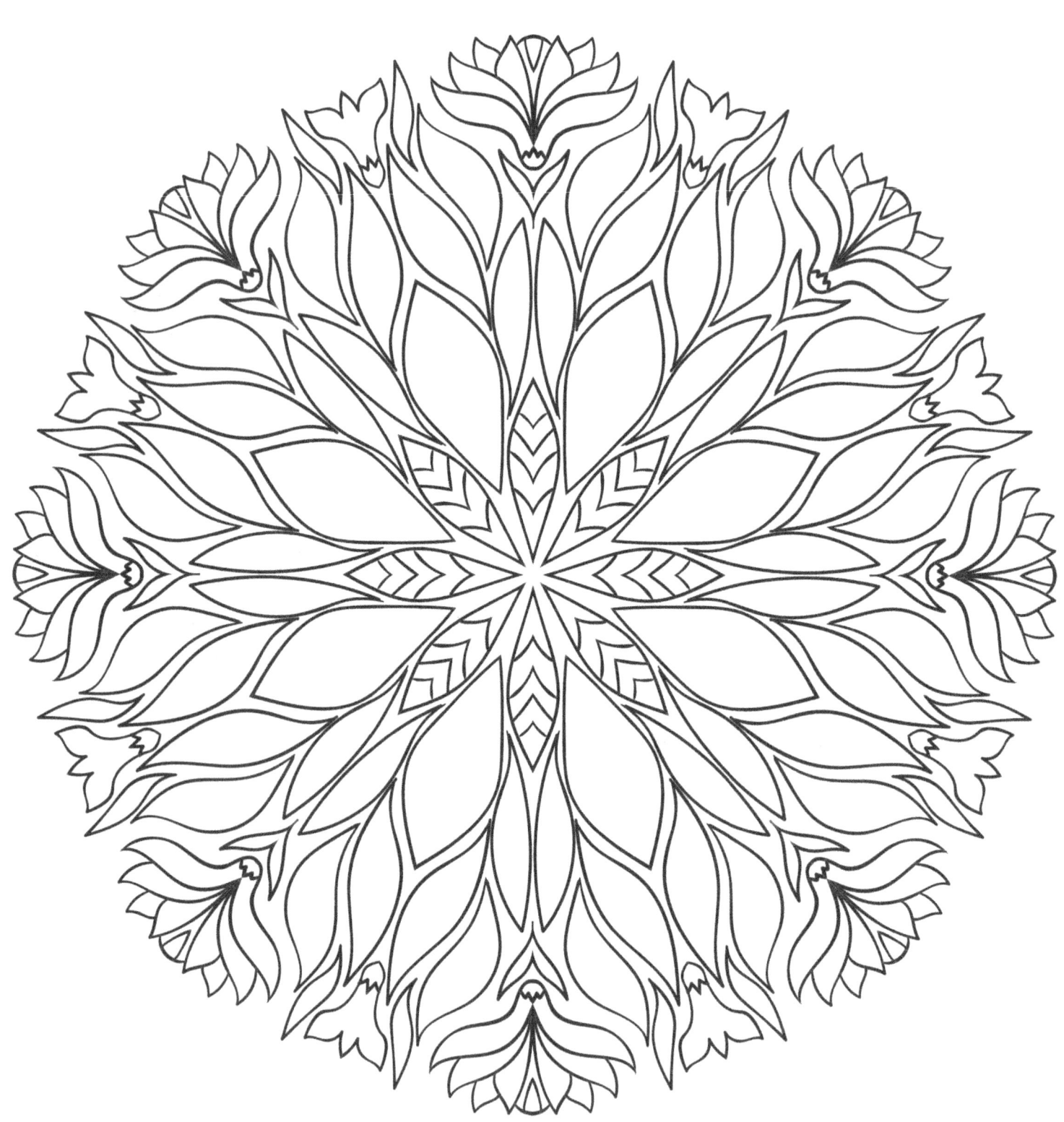

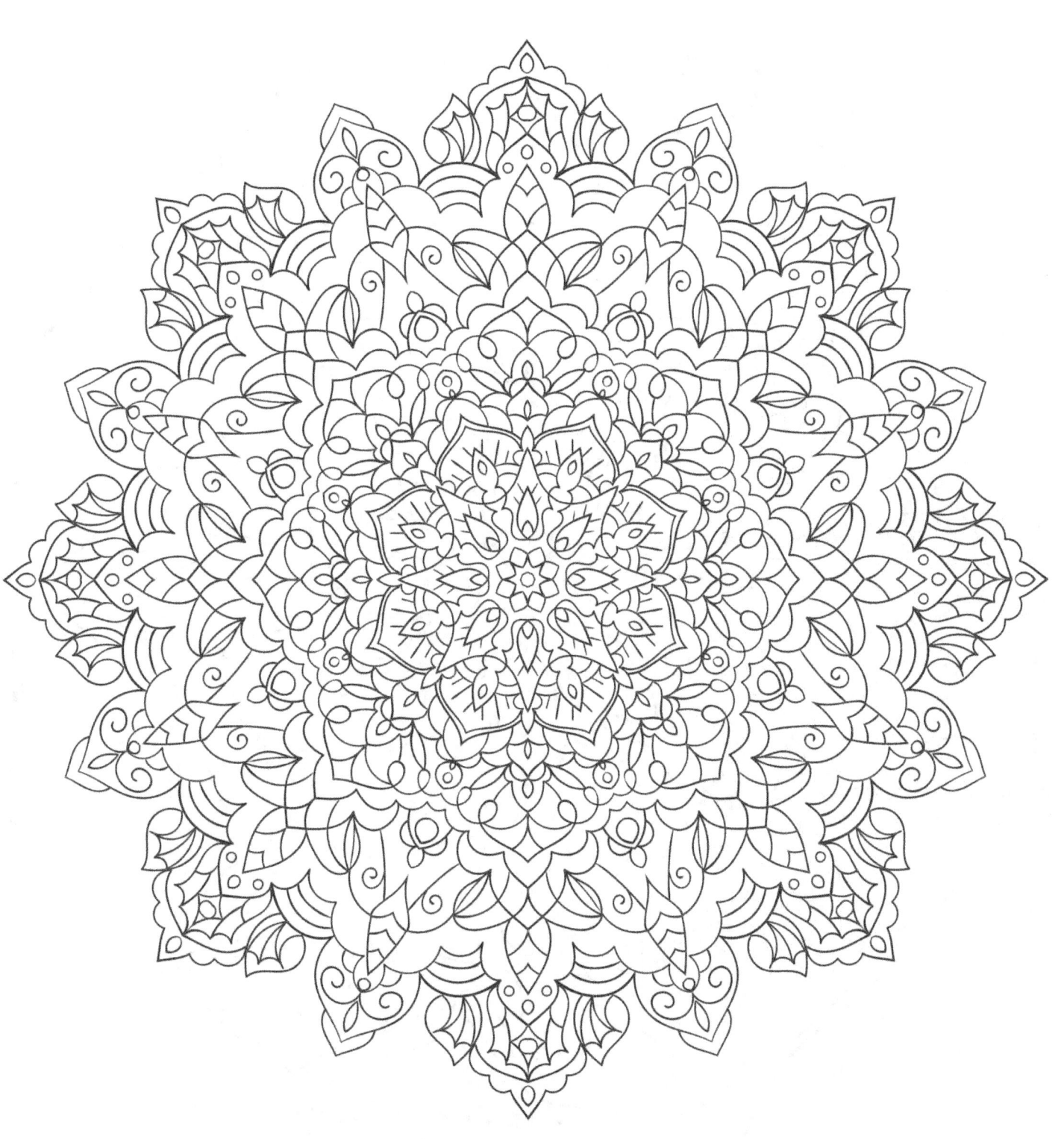

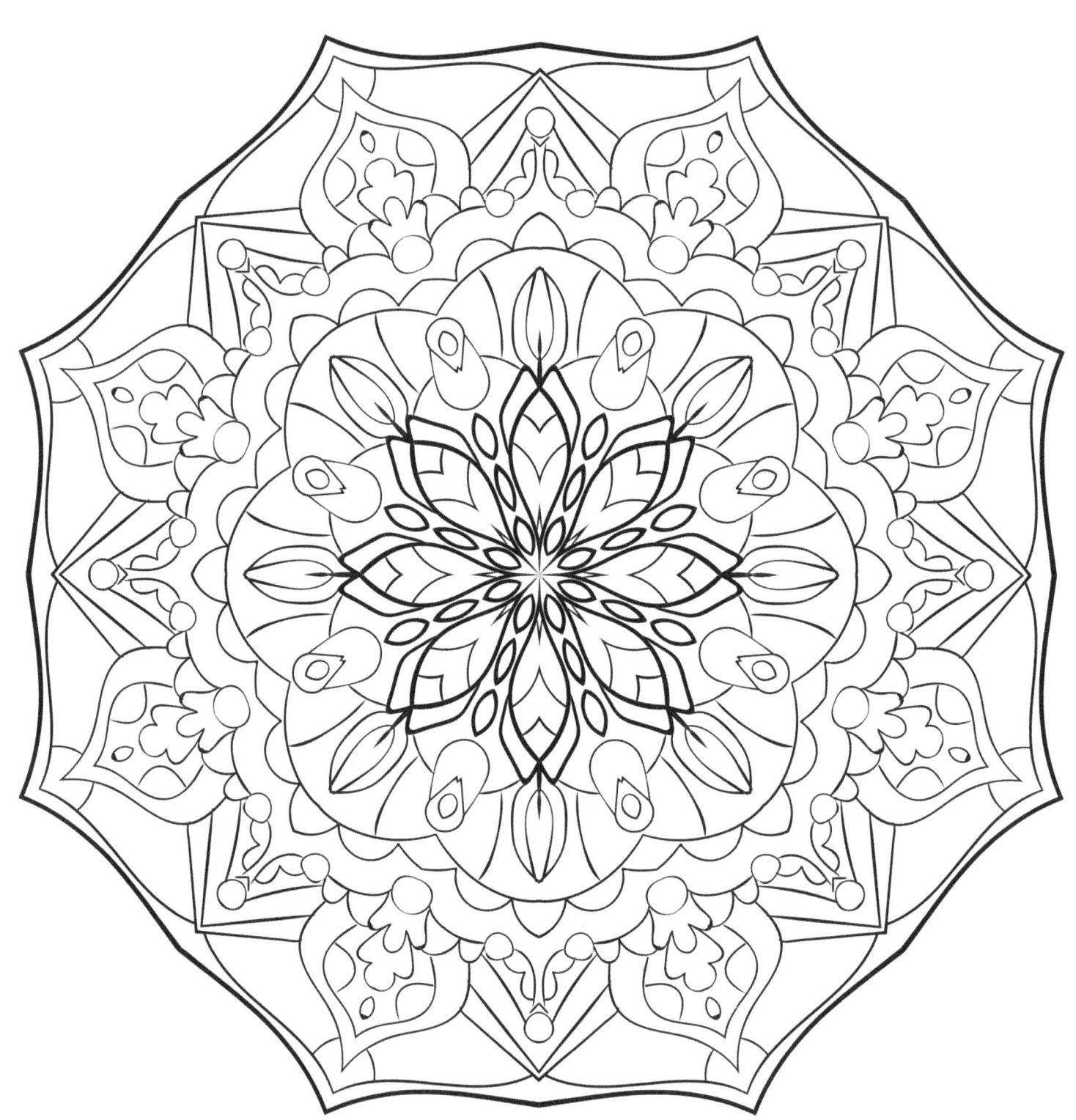

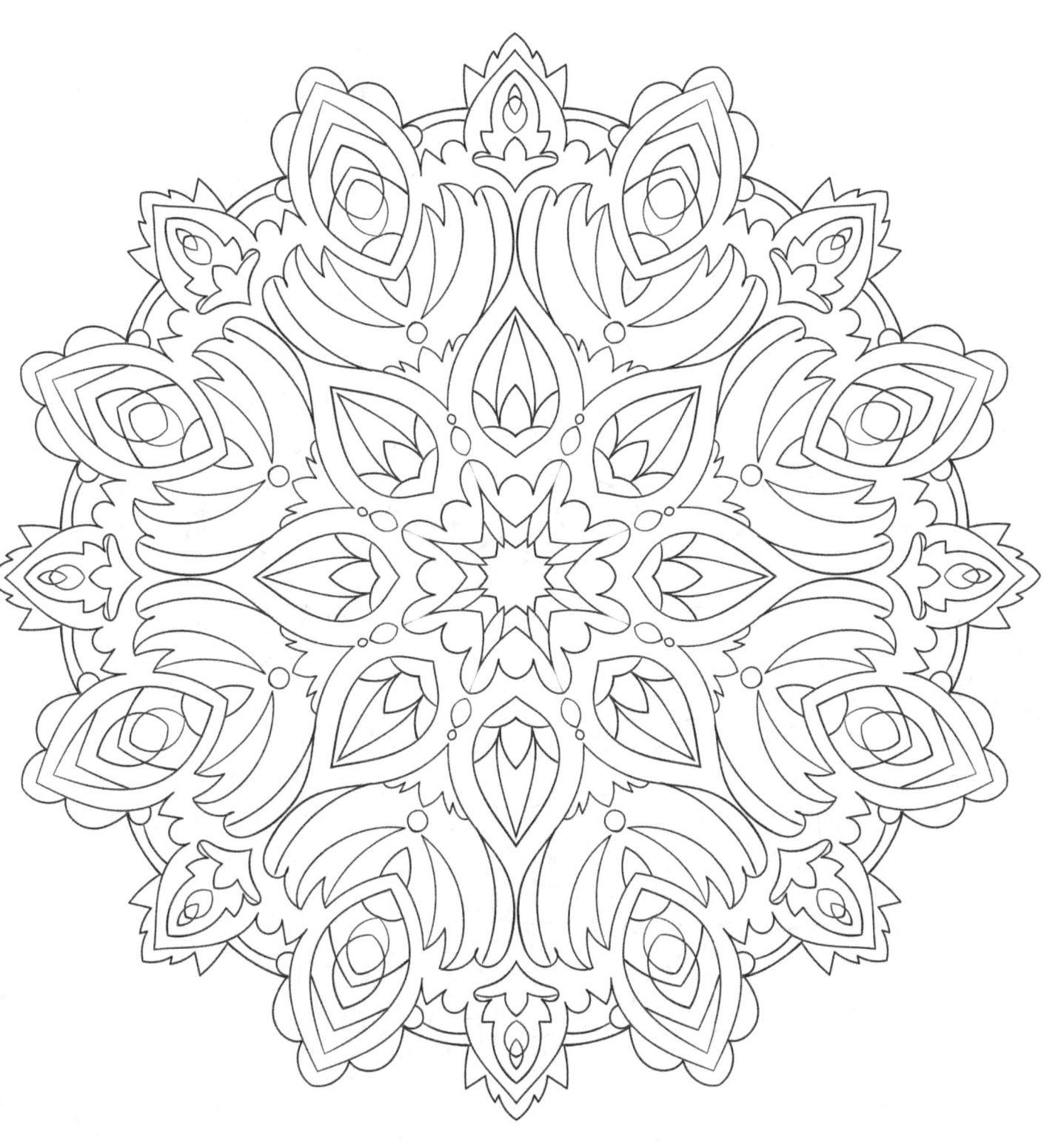

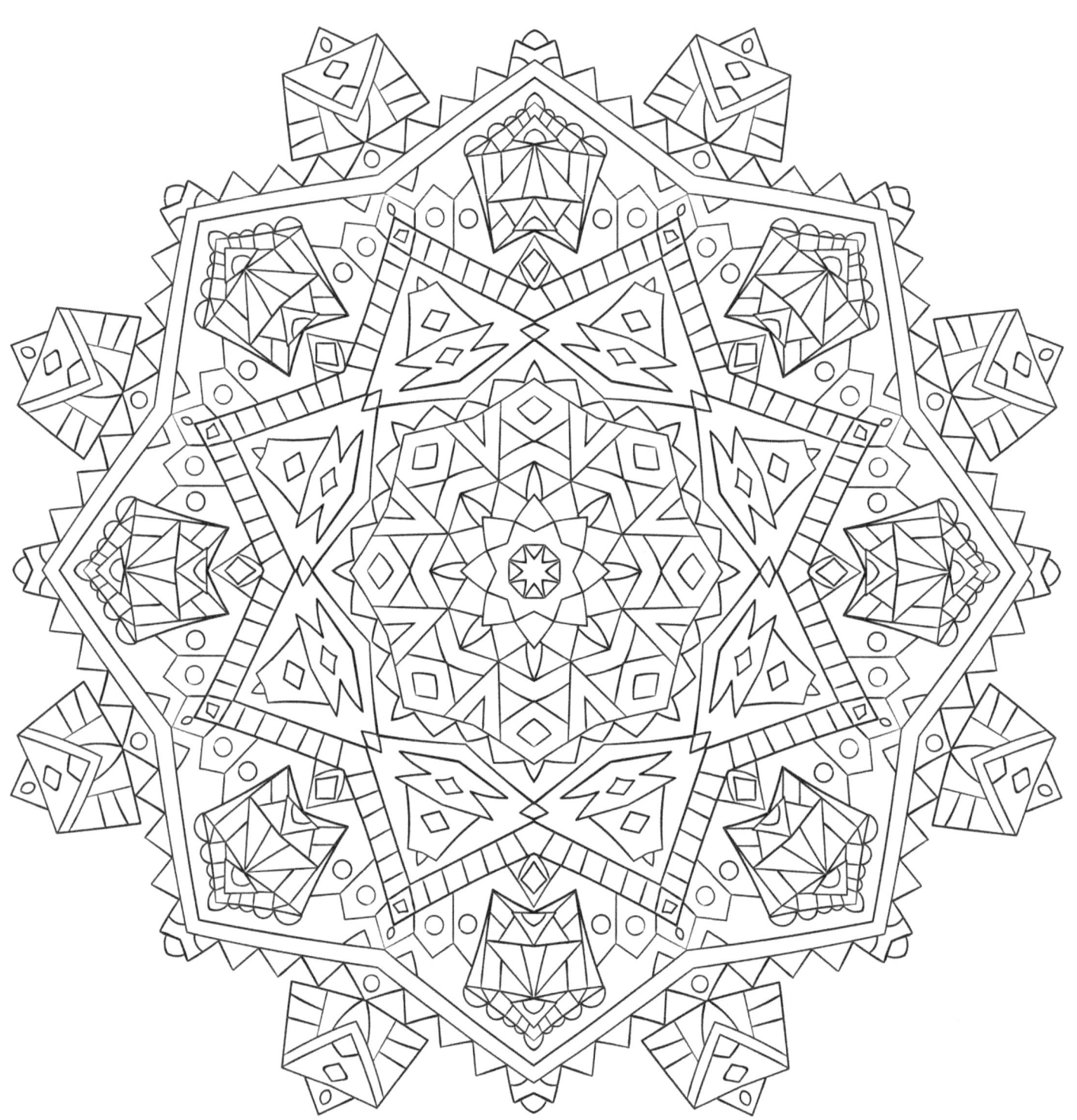

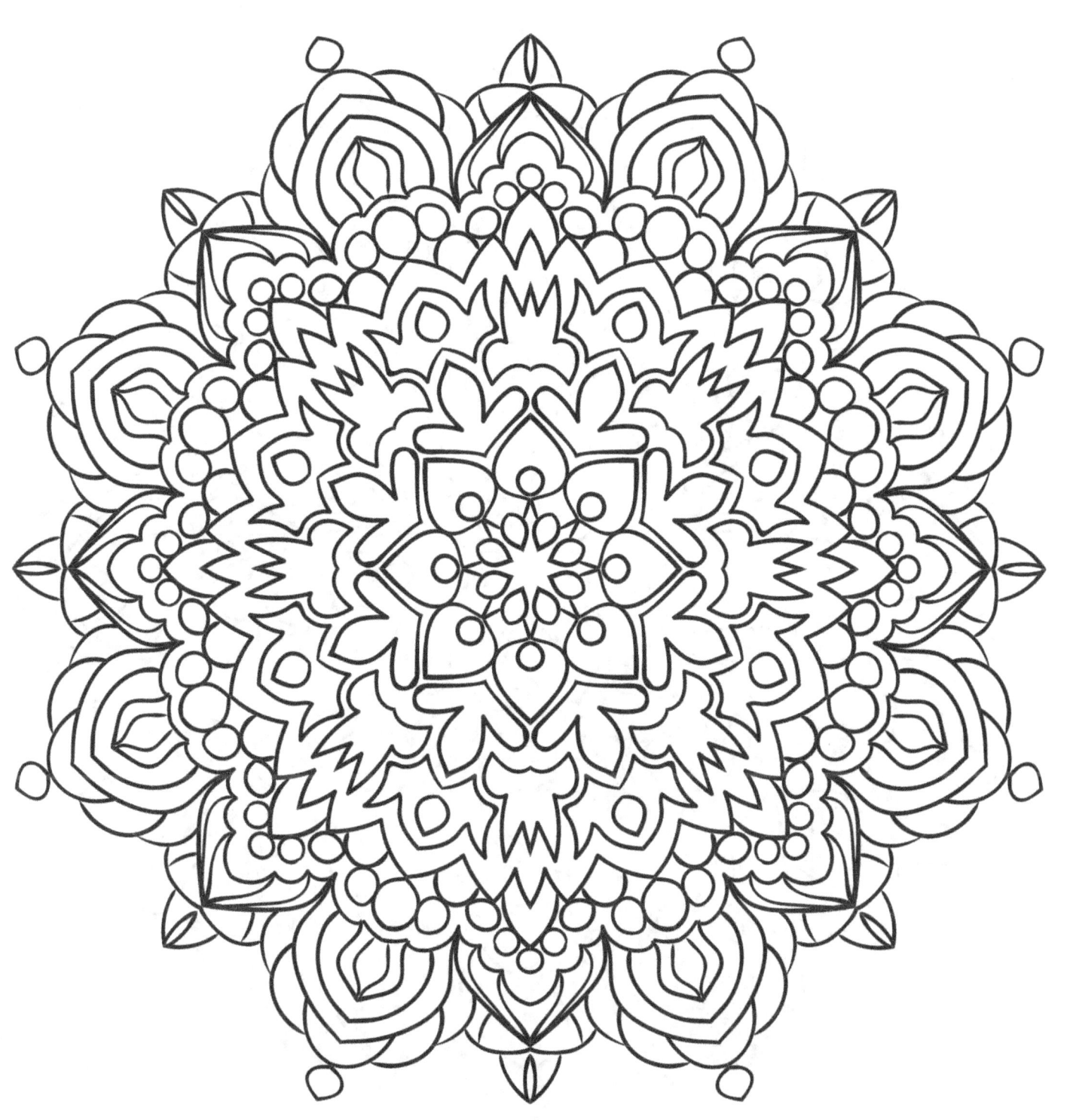

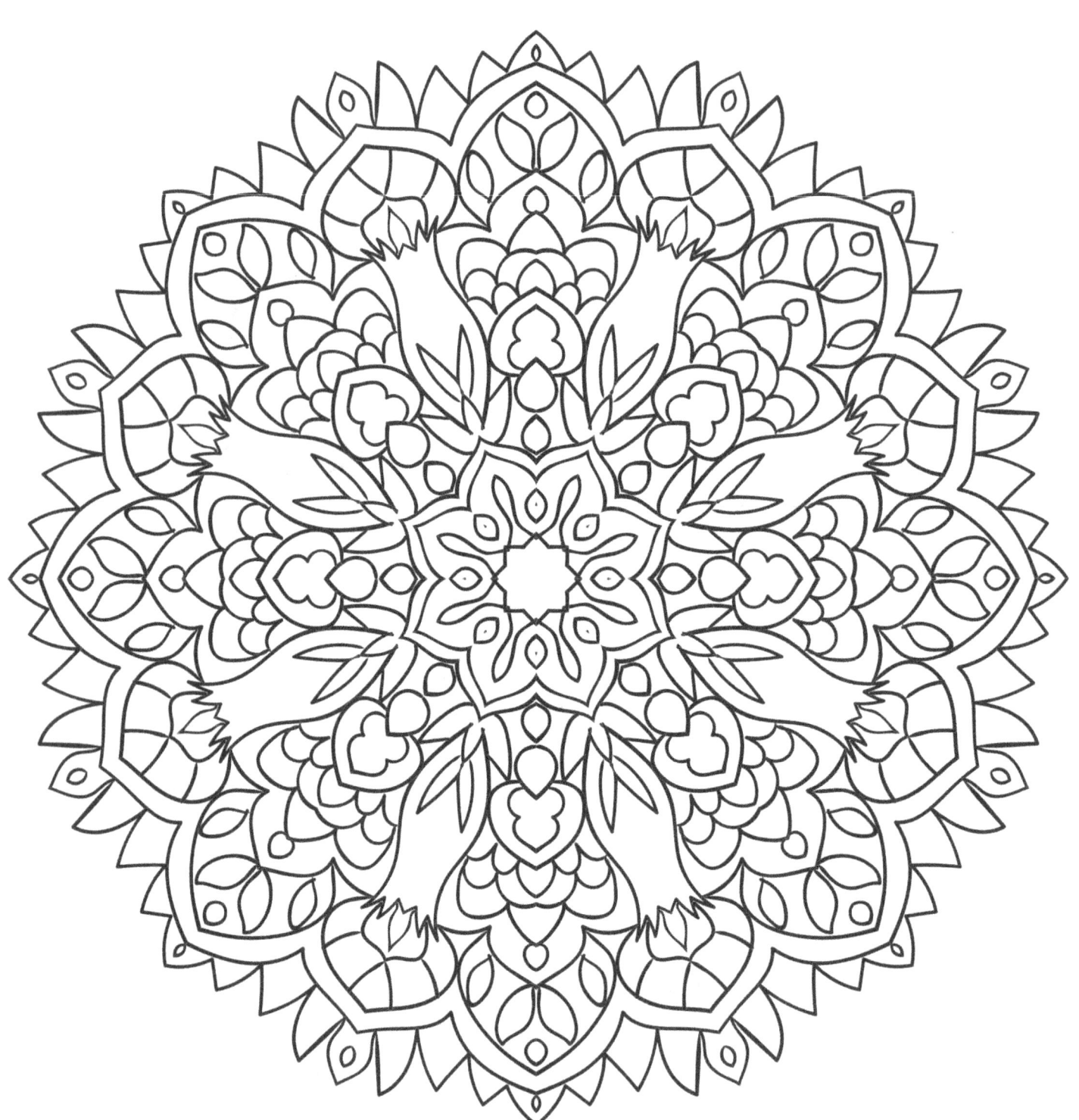